Weddings
& Courtships
France

Love and Romance
The French Way

Lisa Shea

Cover design by Lisa Shea

Book design by Lisa Shea

Nearly all photographs in this book were taken by Lisa Shea and Bob See on one of their trips to France. The French toast and croquembouche images are stock photography. If you have any questions about our own photos, where we took them or the background of the image, let us know!

- v1 -

Visit WeddingsAndCourtships.com for more details about this series.

This is the fully updated front-to-back revised 2015 version of the book I first wrote in 2002.

Print ISBN-13: 978-1508917540

Contents

Introduction 1

French Lovers 3
   Eleanore of Aquitaine 4
   Marie de Champagne and Andreas Capellanus 6
   Heloise and Abelard 9
   Napoleon and Josephine 12

Recipes 14
   Breakfast Croissants 15
   Grand Marnier Crepes 17
   French Toast – Pain Perdu 18
   Traditional French Omelet 19

Wines 20
   Champagne 22
   Burgundy 24
   Chablis 25
   Beaujolais 27
   Red Burgundy 29
   Bordeaux 30
   Sauternes 31
   French Wine Tsating 32
   Beaujolais Nouveau 34
   Wine-Tasting Score Sheet 35

Dating Ideas 36
   Music and Dance 37
   People-Watching 38
   Wine and Cheese 39
   Painting Class 40

Courting 41
   A History of Dating in France 42
   The Colors of Franc 44
   Flowers and Their Meanings 45

Music and Song 48
Love Poetry 50
Words and Phrases 56

Choosing a Mate.. 57
Traditions of Matchmaking..58

The Proposal 59
Engagement Rings 60
Ring Finger 62
The Bridal Trousseau 63

Engagement Traditions 64
Choosing a Wedding Date 65
The Invitation...66
The Fiançailles 68
French Wedding Blessings...69
    1 Corinthians 13 70
Sayings about Marriage..72
Presents 73
The Night Before 74

The Wedding..75
Getting To the Church..76
The Groom 77
Wedding Dress...78
Bridesmaids and Groomsmen 79
Church Decorations..80
The French Ceremony 81
After the Ceremony 82

The Reception 83
Traditions for a Happy Marriage 84
The Garter 85
Decorations and Flowers..86
Music and Dance..87
A French Wedding Cake...88
    Traditional French Wedding Cake Recipe 89
The Wedding Toast 90
Fun Champagne Toasts 91
Clinking of Wine Glasses and Toasts...93
How to Open Champagne 94
Mimosa...96
Kir Royale 97
French 75...98

Chartreuse 99
Champagne & Cheese 100
Champagne & Appetizers 101
Champagne & Desserts 102
Crème Brûlée 104
Madelines 106
Croquembouche 107
French Apple Tart 109

After The Reception 110

Living and Loving the French Way 111
Food and Wine 112
Music and Dining 113
Love and Romance 114
French Hobbies 115
Dandelion Wine 116
French Baby Names 118

French Movies 119

Visiting France 130
Champagne and Reims 131
Paris – City of Love...133
Bordeaux Wine Region 135
Claret Cup 136
Mint Julep 137
Cannes / Beaches of Southern France 138
Monte Carlo and Monaco 139
The Canals of France 141

Glossary of French Terms 142

Web Resources 144
General French Information 144
French Merchants 145
French Travel 146
Champagne Websites 147

Dedication 149

About the Author 150

Weddings
& Courtships
France

Introduction

Love does not consist of gazing at each other but in looking together in the same direction.

—Antoine de Saint-Exupéry

French is often said to be the 'language of love', with its soft murmurings of affection and its loud proclamations of passion. When one thinks of romantic places to visit, the flower-filled streets of Paris spring to mind, with a ride down the river and a walk down the music-filled streets. France is the birthplace of the ideals of courtly love. Eleanor of Aquitaine encouraged that the rules and regulations of courtly love be written down and promoted back in the 1100s.

Many centuries later, modern society equates passionate kissing with the French, dabs itself with French perfumes, and applauds the talents of French clothing designers to bring out the beauty in women of all ages. Champagne is a must at any celebration of love, from the engagement to the wedding to the celebration of new children. Lovers everywhere read romantic tales of the brave and sensual French and thrill to movies about the Three Musketeers and the Moulin Rouge.

Pour yourself a glass of Champagne and raise a toast to the romantic love of France!

A votre Santé—To your Health!

A note for those who buy this in paperback form – Bob and I took all of the photos shown here on our various trips to France. The photos are in full color in all ebook versions of the book. When you buy the paperback version you should gain automatic access to the ebook version of it as well. Even if you don't have a Kindle, you should still be able to download a Kindle app for your PC, phone, or other device, and see the photos that way.

Enjoy!

French Lovers

*"You have been the first among my joys
and you shall be the last,
so long as there is life in me."*
—Bernart de Ventadour

(a minstrel who loved Eleanor of Aquitaine)

France has a long history of famous people involved in deeply romantic situations. The French people are passionate, and love to see that passion reflected in those around them. Many of the underlying foundations of our modern ideals of love were shaped in the French culture. While other cultures built a tradition around arranged marriages, the French idolized the free choice of a man and woman, and the passion and strength of their love. For the French, love and romance were an every-day event, and even older couples can be seen holding hands and flirting with each other.

May the strength and passion of your love burn as true as the passionate couples of France's history!

Eleanore of Aquitaine

Eleanor was born in 1122 to a noble family and was groomed for greatness. She was a woman of great beauty and wit, and many sought her hand in marriage. Many movies and stories have been written about her, including The Lion in Winter with Katherine Hepburn and Peter O'Toole, which tells of her later years as Queen of England. Eleanor encouraged art, poetry, and music about love, and it is her court that first promoted the ideals of courtly love.

At age fifteen, she caught a prize husband—Prince Louis, who became Louis VII, the King of France. She was the Queen of France from 1137-1152. Only four years after her marriage she went to the cathedral of Vezelay and promised the church thousands of her warriors for the crusades. She rode as an amazon with her troops, wearing armor and carrying weapons. Her men adored and fought valiantly for her, but many of the nobility felt her proper place was at home. She ignored them proudly and used her keen intellect to strategize with her generals.

Eleanor warned her husband against trying to take Jerusalem. She instead wanted to go with her uncle, whom she adored, to recapture Edessa. Louis refused and forced Eleanor to go with him against Jerusalem. They failed to take Jerusalem, Eleanor's favorite uncle died, and Eleanor became deeply upset. The couple had two children, but soon Eleanor divorced Louis and took back her lands. A year later, at age thirty, she married Henry of Anjou, an Englishman. He was only twenty at the time, and quite fiery and impetuous, while she was a skilled strategist and planner. Two years after that, in 1154, she was the Queen of England.

The marriage was at first passionate and loving, but after eight children, Eleanor became disheartened with Henry's poor campaign decisions, his numerous affairs, and her own lack of power. Finally, Eleanor sided with her favorite son—Richard the Lionhearted—to try to overthrow Henry. She failed. When she was fifty her husband put her into a comfortable but secure seclusion. It is this period that is portrayed in the movie *The Lion in Winter*.

Luckily for Eleanor, Henry only lived another fifteen years. When her son, Richard, took on the kingship, she was released and took the reins. She managed the kingdom for him while he fought in the Crusades, and traveled extensively throughout Europe until her death in 1204 at the age of eighty-one.

CDarie de Champagne and Andreas Capellanus

Marie de Champagne was the daughter of Eleanor of Aquitaine and King Louis VII. She was raised in the courts of France and shared her mother's passion for courtly love and elegant music. She married Henri I who was also fond of literature and poetry, and between the two of them they helped encourage a culture of reading and music at the court of Poitiers. Marie was the patron of Chretien de Troyes and Andreas Capellanus.

Andreas Capellanus actually means "Andrew the Chaplain." Andreas was fond of Marie and wrote many poems and much prose for her. At her bidding, he wrote a brilliant document on courtly manners entitled "De Amore", or "Of Love." It explained in a very witty way how a proper courtier should act in all matters regarding love.

This three part series included basic definitions of love, sample ways of speaking to a potential lover, and even a long list of 'rules' for love. Here is one of Andreas' statements on love:

"Too great an abundance of passion impedes love, for there are those who are so enslaved by desire that they cannot be restrained by the bonds of love; those who after deep thoughts of their lady or even having enjoyed the fruits of love, when they see another immediately desire her embraces, forget the services received from their former lover and reveal their ingratitude."

While it is true all's fair in love and war, to truly love you must strive to care tenderly for your love. That way love's blossom will ever bloom!

The following Rules of Love were written by Andreas in 1186. Many believe them still true to this day.

Marriage is no excuse for not loving.

He who is not jealous cannot love.

No one can be bound by two loves.

Love is always growing or diminishing.

It is not good for one lover to take anything against the will of the other.

A male cannot love until he has fully reached puberty.

Two years of mourning for a dead lover are prescribed for surviving lovers.

No one should be deprived of love without a valid reason.

No one can love who is not driven to do so by the power of love.

Love always departs from the dwelling place of avarice.

It is not proper to love one whom one would be ashamed to marry.

The true lover never desires the embraces of any save his lover.

Love rarely lasts when it is revealed.

An easy attainment makes love contemptible; a difficult one makes it more dear.

Every lover turns pale in the presence of his beloved.

When a lover suddenly has sight of his beloved, his heart beats wildly.

A new love expels an old one.

Moral integrity alone makes one worthy of love.

If love diminishes, it quickly leaves and rarely revives.

A lover is always fearful.

True jealousy always increases the effects of love.

If a lover suspects another, jealousy and the effects of love increase.

He who is vexed by the thoughts of love eats little and seldom sleeps.

Every action of a lover ends in the thought of his beloved.

The true lover believes only that which he thinks will please his beloved.

Love can deny nothing to love.

A lover can never have enough of the embraces of his beloved.

The slightest suspicion incites the lover to suspect the worst of his beloved.

He who suffers from an excess of passion is not suited to love.

The true lover is continuously obsessed with the image of his beloved.

Nothing prevents a woman from being loved by two men, or a man from being loved by two women.

Ɖeloise and Aɓelard

Heloise (1101-1164) was twenty years younger than Abelard (1079-1142), but this did not stop them from falling passionately in love with each other. She was the daughter of a well-to-do family, and he was a famous, well established philosopher. When they met and fell in love, Abelard moved in with Heloise's family under the pretext of helping to educate her. Heloise was intelligent, beautiful, and quite a match for his intellect.

Heloise's guardian at the time was her uncle, the canon of the church. It was not long before he found out about their affair. He angrily kicked Abelard out of the house. The uncle was too late, however—Heloise was already pregnant. Heloise went to Abelard's sister's house to have the child, named Astrolabe.

Abelard finally convinced the uncle to let the couple marry, as they now had a child and still loved each other. Heloise refused at first, worried about her uncle's reaction despite the uncle's consent. Soon they ran off and secretly married. Heloise hid out at a nunnery afterwards while the couple tried to think of a way to move on with their lives. Heloise's family, thinking Abelard had abandoned her and forced her into nunhood, took Abelard by force and castrated him.

Seeing the destruction that their relationship had caused, Heloise and Abelard became nun and monk. They continued to love one another from a distance, and wrote letters to each other until they died.

The road of true love is not always smooth, but a true bond cannot be denied!

Here are extracts from the first letter that Heloise wrote to Abelard, in response to the first he sent her after they entered their respective Houses of God.

Your letter written to a friend for his comfort, beloved, was lately brought to me by chance. Seeing at once from the title that it was yours, I began the more ardently to read it in that the writer was so dear to me, that I might at least be refreshed by his words as by a picture of him whose presence I have lost.

For who among kings or philosophers could equal thee in fame? What kingdom or city or village did not burn to see thee? Who, I ask, did not hasten to gaze upon thee when thou appearedst in public, nor on thy departure with straining neck and fixed eye follow thee? What wife, what maiden did not yearn for thee in thine absence, nor burn in thy presence? What queen or powerful lady did not envy me my joys and my bed? There were two things, I confess, in thee especially, wherewith thou couldst at once captivate the heart of any woman; namely the arts of making songs and of singing them. ... It was on this account chiefly that women sighed for love of thee. And as the greater part of thy songs descanted of our love, they spread my fame in a short time through many lands, and inflamed the jealousy of many against me. For what excellence of mind or body did not adorn thy youth? What woman who envied me then does not my calamity now compel to pity one deprived of such delights? What man or women, albeit an enemy at first, is not now softened by the compassion due to me?

Give thy attention, I beseech thee, to what I demand; and thou wilt see this to be a small matter and most easy for thee. While I am cheated of thy presence, at least by written words, whereof thou hast an abundance, present to me the sweetness of thine image. .... When thou hastenedst to God, I followed thee in the habit, nay preceded thee. For as though mindful of the wife of Lot, who looked back from behind him, thou deliveredst me first to the sacred garments and monastic profession before thou gavest thyself to God. And for that in this one thing thou shouldst have had little trust in me I vehemently grieved and was ashamed. For I (God wot) would without hesitation precede or follow thee to the Vulcanian fires according to thy word. For not with me was my heart, but with thee. But now, more than ever, if it be not with thee, it is nowhere. For without thee it cannot anywhere exist. ... While with thee I enjoyed carnal pleasures, many were uncertain whether I did so from love or from desire. But now the end shews in what spirit I began. I have forbidden myself all pleasures that I might obey thy will. I have reserved nothing for myself, save this, to be now entirely thine.

And so in His Name to whom thou has offered thyself, before God I beseech thee that in whatsoever way thou canst thou restore to me thy presence, to wit by writing me some word of comfort. To this end alone that, thus refreshed, I may give myself with more alacrity to the service of God. When in time past thou soughtest me out for temporal pleasures, thou visitedst me with endless letters, and by frequent songs didst set thy Heloise on the lips of all men. With me every public place, each house resounded. How more rightly shouldst thou excite me now towards God, whom thou excitedst then to desire. Consider, I beseech thee, what thou owest me, pay heed to what I demand; and my long letter with a brief ending I conclude. Farewell, my all.

Napoleon and Josephine

Napoleon (1769-1821) entered French military school at the age of nine. At age sixteen he joined the French army as a second lieutenant. He helped quiet a number of revolts, and did extremely well, rising quickly through the ranks. By age twenty-four he was Brigadier General.

Josephine was born in 1763 with the name Rose Tascher, to a noble family from Martinique. Her first husband, joined to her in an arranged marriage, became a general but was killed when she was thirty-one. She enjoyed her life as a worldly and sought-after widow. She met Napoleon in 1795 and was mildly attracted to him. He seemed a bit scruffy to her, and he was eight years her junior. To him she was a 'real woman', not a classic beauty, and he adored her.

Their fondness grew and they became lovers. Napoleon married Josephine in 1796. Several days after the wedding he was sent to the French-Italian border. Although he was given weak troops, he prevailed, and returned a hero. They shared several years of intense, passionate, jealous love before the jealousy overtook them and the relationship disintegrated. Eventually, when she did not bear any sons, which Napoleon demanded for an heir, they annulled their marriage.

He remarried, but she did not. When Josephine died in 1814, he went to her garden and picked some violets—her favorite flower. He wore them in a locket over his heart until he died. True love, they say, never dies. Perhaps you could carry a flower or a lock of your love's hair in a locket over your heart as a token of your affection!

Napoleon and Josephine are very famous for the love letters they left behind. They included the following:

December 1795, Napoleon to Josephine:

I awake full of you. Your image and the memory of last night's intoxicating pleasures has left no rest to my senses.

Sweet, incomparable Josephine, what a strange effect you have on my heart. Are you angry? Do I see you sad? Are you worried? My soul breaks with grief, and there is no rest for your lover; but how much the more when I yield to this passion that rules me and drink a burning flame from your lips and your heart? Oh! This night has shown me that your portrait is not you!

You leave at midday; in three hours I shall see you.

Meanwhile, my sweet love, a thousand kisses; but do not give me any, for they set my blood on fire.

B.

April 1796, Napoleon to Josephine:

I have your letters of the 16th and 21st. There are many days when you don't write. What do you do, then? No, my darling, I am not jealous, but sometimes worried. Come soon; I warn you, if you delay, you will find me ill. Fatigue and your absence are too much.

Your letters are the joy of my days, and my days of happiness are not many. Junot is bringing twenty-two flags to Paris.

You must come back with him, you understand? Hopeless sorrow, inconsolable misery, sadness without end, if I am so unhappy as to see him return alone. Adorable friend, he will see you, he will breathe in your temple; perhaps you will even grant him the unique and perfect favor of kissing your cheek, and I shall be alone and far, far away. But you are coming, aren't you? You are going to be here beside me, in my arms, on my breast, on my mouth? Take wing and come, come!

A kiss on your heart, and one much lower down, much lower! B.

Recipes

"Enchant, stay beautiful and graceful, but do this, eat well. Bring the same consideration to the preparation of your food as you devote to your appearance. Let your dinner be a poem, like your dress."

—Charles Pierre Monselet

Perhaps because the sensual side of the French lover is such a popular image, one of the most romantic French meals is breakfast in bed. Get yourself a pair of lovely bed-trays, find a small vase to hold a single bloom, and plan out a delicious breakfast for you and your lover!

The menu can include:

French Vanilla Tea

Small Traditional French Chocolates

French Breakfast Puffs, Croissants, or Pain Chocolate Crepes

French Toast French Omelet

Read on for recipes to help you plan your own morning romance!

Breakfast Croissants

Croissants are the perfect breakfast bread! This is undeniably French, and can be flavored to please your palate. You can have them in their natural state, with a bit of butter, or you can add chocolate, cheese, or berries. Create your own favorites!

3 1/2 cups unbleached flour
1 cup milk
1/4 cup sugar
1 oz yeast
2 tsp salt
1 lb unsalted butter
1 egg
1 tsp milk

Bring the milk to room temperature. Mix together the flour, milk, sugar, yeast and salt until it forms a dough. Add in more warm milk if the dough is not moist enough. Knead for ten minutes, until smooth. Put into an oiled bowl and cover with a towel for twenty minutes.

Now roll out the dough into a large rectangle, about a half-inch thick. Wrap in plastic and put in the fridge for at least an hour. This section of the dough-making can easily be done the night before.

When you're ready to continue the croissant creation, take out the dough and place it on a flat, floured surface. Roll the chilled rectangle into a quarter-inch thick rectangle. Place a thin layer of butter over the top of this rectangle – you can either roll the butter out very thin, slice it into thin slices or even melt it and brush it over the top. Fold the dough in half lengthwise. Roll out into a rectangle about ten inches by fifteen. Now fold this into thirds by folding the top down two-thirds of the way and then folding the bottom up.

Wrap again in plastic and chill for another hour. Do this from 3 to 6 times, depending on how layered you want your croissant to be. When you're on the final folding for the night, roll it out to ¼" thick and cut the dough into triangles. Roll each triangle from the fat end towards a point, and then turn in the corners to give it a crescent shape.

The morning that you'll eat the croissants, mix together the egg and milk, and brush this over the tops of your croissants. First put them into an oven at about 200°F for 1 ½ hours, with a pan of water in the bottom. This will steam them and get them ready for cooking. Now heat the oven to 400°F and cook for 15 minutes. Serve and enjoy!

Grand Marnier Crepes

These crepes are a lovely morning meal, and best shared with a cup of hot chocolate, coffee or tea!

9 oz milk
2 eggs
2 Tbsp granulated sugar
1 tsp salt
¾ cup flour
1 Tbsp butter
2 oz Grand Marnier

Mix together the milk, eggs, sugar, and salt. Next, add in the flour slowly, until you have a smooth mixture. Melt the butter and add it in. Finally, add the Grand Marnier.

Refrigerate the mixture for at least 2 hours. You can prepare this the night before if you wish. When you're ready to cook, butter a frying pan and pour in a thin layer of the mixture. Cook until just golden on either side, and serve warm.

Crepes are the perfect vehicle for your favorite sweets! Spread a crepe onto a plate for preparation. You can paint on a layer of powdered sugar, honey, jam, chocolate sauce, whipped cream, or just about any other item you can sprinkle or spread. Roll the circle up into a little log and enjoy!

French Toast - Pain Perdu

French toast was often made by peasants to use up any stale bread left in the house. It's a well-loved dish in many parts of the world now, although in modern days we tend to use fresh bread! It works especially well with French bread and Italian bread.

1 cup milk
4 large eggs
¼ cup sugar
2 tsp vanilla extract
½ tsp nutmeg
8 slices of bread
4 Tbsp butter
4 Tbsp vegetable oil

Blend together milk, eggs, sugar, vanilla, and nutmeg. Soak the bread in the mixture until coated. Put the butter and oil into a frying pan and wait until hot. Put a piece of soaked bread into the pan and fry until golden brown on each side. Place in a 200°F oven to keep warm while you work on the remaining pieces.

French Toast can be served in many ways. Some people enjoy it with maple syrup, others enjoy honey or jam. You can also sprinkle it with powdered sugar and cinnamon, and slice it into halves or triangles.

Traditional French Omelet

The Omelet has become part of many breakfast traditions, but it traces back to the French. This versatile dish can be a simple breakfast, a delicious lunch, even a tasty dinner, all depending on what ingredients you use.

3 eggs
1 Tbsp milk
1/4 cup cheddar cheese, shredded
1 Tbsp butter
salt & pepper

Mix the eggs and milk together in a bowl with a fork until well blended. Melt the butter in a non-stick skillet (they do sell pans especially for omelets!) until it's fully melted. Pour in the egg mixture and swirl the pan until it's evenly coated. Carefully cook, lifting the edges occasionally to let the still-liquid egg reach the pan surface.

After about a minute the omelet should be mostly cooked. Sprinkle the cheese over one half of the omelet. Flip the other side over to envelop the cheese and cook for another 1/2 minute. Serve hot and spice to your taste.

While this is the most simple of omelet recipes, there are infinite combinations you can use to add more flair to your omelet. These include:

bits of cooked bacon
chopped green peppers
diced tomatoes
chopped mushrooms
small cubes of cooked ham
small bits of onion

Use your imagination, and make up new and interesting omelet combinations!

Wines

"Wine makes a symphony of a good meal."

—Fernande Garvin

While many people are quite comfortable choosing wines from California or Australia, it can be very confusing to choose wines from France. Where wines from many regions of the world are identified with the grape type – Chardonnay, Cabernet Sauvignon – wines from France often only tell you the wine region and assume you know the rest.

Never fear! Read on about the different wines in France, and do some shopping around. You will find that you can get delicious wines on any budget, and you might find either a new inexpensive house wine, or a new favorite for special evenings together!

First, here's a chart to help you understand where specific wines are made.

Wine	Region	Main Grapes
Banyuls	Pyrenees	Grenache
Beaujolais	Burgundy	gamay
Bordeaux	Bordeaux	cabernet sauvignon, merlot, etc.
Chablis	Burgundy	chardonnay
Champagne	Champagne	chardonnay, pinot noir, etc.
Chartreuese	Vauvert	wine base
Côte d'Or	Burgundy	pinot noir, chardonnay
Macon	Burgundy	pinot blanc, chardonnay, etc.
Medoc	Bordeaux	cabernet sauvignon, merlot, etc.
Muscadet	Loire Valley	melon de Bourgogne
Sancerre	Loire Valley	sauvignon blanc, pinot noir
Sauternes	Bordeaux	Semillon, cabernet, muscadelle
Vouvray	Loire Valley	chenin blanc

Champagne

Champagne is a region of France, and only wines which come from this region can properly be called "Champagne." Similar drinks from California and the rest of the world should be called "sparkling wines."

Champagne's signature bubbles were originally a happy accident! Back in the 1700s, wine was supposed to be flat, like most wine is today. Bubbles were an error in the process, and the monk Dom Pérignon worked hard to remove them. Instead, he found methods of blending and clarifying the drink, and soon it was sought after by the French aristocracy. The rest, they say, is history!

Champagne is made using the *Methode Champenoise*, which requires two fermentations. This is different from normal, "still" wines, which only go through one fermentation. Here's a quick description of how a Champagne is created.

The first, and most important part of any wine is the grapes. Sparkling Wine grapes are grown just as any other grape is— carefully tended and cared for. When fall comes, the grapes are gently harvested.

The grapes used in sparkling wines are typically Chardonnay, Pinot Noir, Pinot Meunier and Pinot Gris. Some Champagnes are made solely with Chardonnay.

The wine is fermented in a stainless steel tank. It ferments for two to three weeks, and then sits for up to five months. It is at this point that the process diverts from the normal winemaking process.

When the winemaker decides the wine is ready, it is bottled with extra sugar and yeast, and capped with a soda-cap. The wine is allowed to ferment from one to three years or more. When this second fermentation and resting period are over, the yeast and sediment must be removed from the bottle.

The bottles are put into a riddling rack, which slowly rotates the wine from a horizontal position up to a vertical one. This allows the sediment from the second fermentation to slowly slide down into the neck of the bottle, for easy removal.

The removal process is called *disgorgement*. The neck of the bottle is inserted into a machine, which freezes it. When the cap is removed, the frozen plug at the neck is removed. A "dosage" of Champagne is added to fill in the space in the bottle, and it is corked with the standard, large Champagne cork.

Note that the cork does not start out in its mushroom-like shape— it starts out as a straight 'tube' shape. It is only the pressure and system of corking that gives it its broad head and flared bottom.

Champagne is stored for drinking just like any other wine – preferably at around 55°F, in a dark, damp location, stored on its side to keep the cork from drying out. Champagne should be served at about 45° F. A few hours in the refrigerator should bring the temperature down, but never store any wine for more than a few days in the refrigerator. It can harm a wine in the same way that storing it at 100°F would.

Serve your Champagne in tall, narrow-necked glasses, called flutes. Do not use wide-brimmed glasses—they cause the drink to quickly lose both bubbles and flavor.

There are different types of Champagne. Brut is the driest, and the "standard." If you want to enjoy a "great" Champagne, go for a Brut. Extra-dry is less dry than Brut. Sec is sweet, and Demi Sec is even sweeter.

Vintage bottles are, like most wines, from a single year's worth of grapes. Unlabeled or non-vintage bottles are from a blend of several years.

For related wines, note that Spain calls its wines of this type Cava, or Cellar. South Africa uses the term Cap Classique or Cape Classic. Germany has Sekt, and of course there's always Asti Spumanti from Italy!

Burgundy

Many of the names wine drinkers associate with France come from Burgundy. These include Chablis, Beaujolais, Macon, Côte de Beaune, Côte d'Or. Located in eastern France, below Paris, Burgundy is often the sole stop of wine drinkers touring this country.

Burgundy is known as Bourgogne in France, and has a long history of winemaking. Each sub-region of Burgundy has its own unique character, so it is hard to address the region as a whole, and to make any sweeping generalities. The flinty, classic Chablis flavor is made solely with Chardonnay grapes, while the freshness of Beaujolais Nouveau comes from the fruity Gamay.

Read on to learn more about the three main types of Burgundian wines – Chablis, Beaujolais and "Burgundy" – also known as Pinot Noir.

Chablis

Chablis wines come only from the Chablis section of Burgundy, France, which is in the north of Burgundy. Chablis is a white wine, made from the Chardonnay grape.

These grapes are grown in a very flinty soil—visitors to the area are often surprised by the rocky quality of this landscape. It is this "Kimmeridgian" limestone that gives Chablis its distinct flavor.

Chablis was first "wined" back in the 500's—a monastery was built there, and invading Romans brought along wine wherever they went. When Charlemagne set up a base here, it was very important that wine be offered to visiting guests. By the 1400's Chablis was a well-known region, but it fell to war and fighting in the 1600's. Just as it recovered from these, it was hit by the phylloxera troubles that affected just about every other region of the continent. Phylloxera was a louse which destroyed the roots of grapevines, which almost wiped out all grape vines in Europe.

Chablis was set aside as an Appellation d'origine around 1937. There are approximately 7,500 acres of land in the Chablis region, and the four appellations there are based on the type of land where the vines are grown. There are:

Chablis Grand Cru: the north bank of the Serein river

Chablis Premier Cru: south—and west-facing hills

Chablis: north—and east-facing hills

Petit Chablis: flat ground

There are only seven Grand Cru vineyards: Les Clos, Blanchots, Bougros, Vaudésir, Valmur, Preuses, and Grenouilles. There are around forty Premier Crus, with some smaller vineyards falling under the name of a larger group. For example, Chapelot, Pied d'Aloue, and Cote de Brechain all fall under the name 'Montee de Tonnerre'.

A Premier Chablis should be aged for around 10 years, and served at about 52°F (11°C). These wines go well with seafood (especially oysters) and light poultry. Chablis are typically light, crisp, fruity, and floral. They have a bit of a steely edge to their flavor.

Beaujolais

How does a region choose a grape? Back in July 1395, the "Gamay" grape was forbidden to be used in Burgundy. Beaujolais, the southern neighbor, decided it should use Gamay and make its wines from this grape. Thus started a differentiation that continues to this day. Today, 98% of this region is planted with Gamay grapes; the rest is Pinot Noir and Chardonnay.

The Beaujolais region is comprised of 55,000 acres, more than the three other regions of Burgundy combined. Beaujolais itself is split in two by the Nizerand River. North is Haut-Beaujolais with light soil. This produces the Beaujolais-Villages wines and all ten Crus. South of the river are the Bas-Beaujolais.

Beaujolais is very light, fruity, and easy to drink. It typically has aromas of pear and banana. Because of its easy drinkability, there is a lot of cheap, jug wine—normally served in 46 cl containers. On the other hand, the Crus also produce fine quality, crafted wines. Beaujolais Nouveau is the first output from each harvest—ready exactly on the Third Thursday of November each year. It's a celebration across the world, as people gather to taste the first Beaujolais of the new season.

Around half of all Beaujolais wine is Bas Beaujolais, at 10% alcohol. A small amount is Beaujolais Superieur, 10.5% alcohol. One quarter is Beaujolais-Villages, and the remainder is split beteween other varietals. Beaujolais has a distinct wine making method—a combination of carbonic maceration and chaptalization, or adding sugar to boost the alcohol content.

Beaujolais owes much of its fame to Georges Duboeuf, who promoted it far and wide. He controls 10% of Beaujolais production. Louis Jadot also creates a fine wine.

How long can you keep a Beaujolais? Beaujolais Nouveau should be drunk *immediately*—it is barely even wine, being released so soon after the harvest. Most Beaujolais and Beaujolais-Villages should be drunk within 2 years. Some of the best crus can last 3, and some made in more 'traditional' winemaking styles could last up to 10 years if it's a really good vintage.

Red Burgundy

The Côte d'Or is located in the very heart of Burgundy, France. The literal translation of Côte d'Or is "golden slope", but the name is actually an abbreviation for *Cote d'Orient*, or "east slope." This region stretches for a narrow 35 mile band.

The Côte d'Or has two primary sections. First, the northerly Côte de Nuits, grows mainly Pinot Noir and other red grapes. This half is named for the village Nuits-Saint-Georges, and is a mere one mile by 12 miles.

Second, the southerly Côte de Beaune, which, while well known for its white wines, actually grows both Chardonnay and red grapes. The land in the Cote is mostly limestone, which produces high quality wines. One of the most famous villages in the Côte de Beaune is Pommard, known for its heavy, full-bodied red wine.

There are also other, smaller areas in the Côte d'Or. To the far north is the Châtillon region, centered around Châtillon-sur-Seine. This area makes both red and white wines, as well as a *Crémant de Bourgogne*, or Champagne-style sparkler.

On the hills behind the Côte lay the Hautes-Côtes vineyards. These have been seeing more and more winemaking effort in the past few years.

The Côte d'Or has restrictions on yields to preserve quality. The maximum yield for most vineyards here is 40 hl/ha of red, or 45 hl/ha of white. Most wines from the Côte d'Or are matured for a year to 18 months in oak barrels. The top wines from the Côte d'Or are the Grand Crus—there are 32 of them. Next come the Premier Crus, then Villages, and finally regionals.

Bordeaux

The region of Bordeaux, France is the largest wine growing region in the world. Bordeaux is comprised of five main districts— Medoc, St. Emilion, Pomerol, Graves, and Sauternes. While Medoc and the entire region are best known for their reds ("Clarets"), white wines also have their place. The Graves region creates dry whites, and Sauternes is known for its sweet white wines.

Bordeaux is divided by the Gironde River and the Garonne River. To the west, or "left bank", lies the capital city of Bordeaux. The Left Bank is the more well known of the two banks. It contains the Medoc, Graves, Margaux, Pauillac, and Pessac-Léognan regions.

To the east, or "right bank", lie the Pomerol and St-Émilion regions. In the middle of the two is the Entre-Duex-Mers (between two seas) area.

The red Bordeaux wines are created with Cabernet Sauvignon grapes, often blended with Cabernet Franc and Merlot. The color tends to be a garnet/ruby shade. The flavor is typically a light one, with aromas of blackberry, black fruits, and wood. A classic Bordeaux is said to have a "cigar box" aroma to it.

Graves, the dry whites, are made by blending mostly Sauvignon Blanc grapes with a small amount of Sauvignon Gris. Sauternes, the sweeter white wines, are made with Sémillon grapes, Sauvignon and a drop of Muscadelle.

There are many levels of quality of wine grown in Bordeaux, so for the 1855 Exposition Universelle de Paris (sort of like a World Fair) Napoléon III asked a panel to break the region's wines down by price (therefore, hopefully, isolating quality as well). These classifications of 1855 were never meant to be an official quality roster.

The classifications were grouped by region within Bordeaux, and remain mostly unchanged to this day.

Sauternes

Sauternes is a region of Bordeaux, France, well known for its sweet white wines. There are five villages in Graves that make this wine style—Sauternes, Barsac, Preignac, Fargues, and Bommes.

This region is located near a river, and the resulting misty conditions help breed a "noble rot"—pourriture noble. This is a particular kind of mold which causes rich flavors to come out in the grapes it affects. Early winemakers found that this rot turned the flavor of the grapes into a rich, honey flavor, with a deep brown color. Unlike many wines, this wine can age almost indefinitely and still be enjoyed.

Sauternes are primarily made with the semillon grape, along with small amounts of sauvignon and muscadelle.

It is difficult to make a Sauternes. The rot must be of just the right level, and only the most affected grapes are picked. During fermentation, these grapes get up to 14% alcohol in them—this kills off the yeast, leaving behind much of the sugar that normally would be fermented away.

Flavors in sauterne wines range between apricot, peach, pineapple, and vanilla. The wines are smooth and creamy. More so than many other wine types, vintage in Sauternes is extremely important. The weather conditions can make or break an entire year's crop in this region.

"First Great Growth" (Premier Cru Supérieur) of Sauternes-Barsac (1855): Château d'Yquem (Sauternes)

French Wine Tasting

Holding a wine tasting party is thoroughly French, and thoroughly fun. It's also pretty easy if you know the basics.

The saying goes, you use all your senses except hearing to judge a wine. You eye the wine's color. You savor its smell. You both taste it with your mouth, and feel its texture as it swishes across your tongue. And then you contemplate its after effects. To sit by a fire with friends, sipping wine and discussing life ... what could be better?

Remember through all of this, you're figuring out how much you like the wine—this is all highly subjective! As the Wine Spectator magazine discovered, *"When test groups of French and Germans were given wine with 8 grams of sugar per liter, 92 percent of the Germans called the wine "dry" while only 7 percent of the French did. Their reference points were different: German whites are more often frankly sweet than French ones, so the German tasters were less sensitive to sugar in their wines."*

First, gather a few friends and a few bottles of wine. I've found it's best to let each person bring a bottle—you learn about all sorts of new wines you've never heard of before. And each friend has a story about where and when they found this particular brand. Have clean glasses, water, and bread of some sort to cleanse the palate between wines. And set aside lots of time.

Open a bottle of wine. Usually people taste wine from dry to sweet, but do whatever feels good for you group. This is supposed to be fun, after all! Pour each glass maybe a third of the way full. Examine the wine both from the side and top of the glass. How is the color? Is it consistent? Are there bubbles? If there's something white to hold it against, this can help. Always hold the glass by the stem, so your hand doesn't warm up the wine.

Next, swirl the wine around so the edges of the wine just reach the top of the glass. Smell the wine. The swirling motion has released a set of odors—can you recognize anything about them? Something fruity? A berry, perhaps? Or maybe oak or wood? There are a myriad of scents in every bottle of wine. Use your eyes here as well—watch the "tears" of wine that drip back down into the bottom. Also, sometimes a wine that smells strongly of tannins will make the sides of your tongue tingle!

Take maybe a third-of-a-mouthful into your mouth, and swish it around onto every part of your tongue. Your tongue has "zones" for each type of flavor it can taste, so you want the wine to be able to go over each section. The tip senses sweet, the front sides salt, the back sides acid, and the very back bitter. Even in each section, there are buds of different "intensities." Also, examine texture. How does it feel in your mouth? Is the wine fizzy? Viscous? What new flavors can you taste and smell, now that the wine is warming up?

Finally, drink the wine and see what after-flavors continue to appear. Did everything in the wine seem "balanced", or was it too sweet or tart? How long does the aftertaste last?

Make sure that the wine is served at the proper temperature, and into a clean glass. Dish soap in glasses can play havoc with a wine's true taste! If you've recently eaten or drunk anything else, have some bread or something else "neutral" to cleanse your palate.

Beaujolais Nouveau

For a truly authentic French event, be sure to celebrate Beaujolais Nouveau each fall! Beaujolais Nouveau is a celebration of the New Beaujolais—the first wine—of a given year.

It's a party! Beaujolais is a region of France right next to the Burgundy region, and their use of the Gamay grape goes back to July of 1395. This event used to be a reward for the workers, to celebrate the harvest time. The wine is barely fermented and aged before it is poured and served.

This party began to get out of hand as it grew each year, so the French government stepped in to manage it. In 1938 they implemented strict restrictions, but as the tradition grew, these were released, and now it has become a national holiday of sorts. The release is now timed on the morning of the third Thursday of November, and is an international sport—a race to see who can be the very first to try this young wine!

Around two thirds of Beaujolais Nouveau comes from vineyards in the main Beaujolais appellation, or region. The rest of this wine is from the Beaujolais Villages area.

How does this young Beaujolais Nouveau taste? It is a light, fruity wine, best enjoyed when chilled to around 45°F. Try it with turkey, or with brie and edam cheese for a pre-dinner snack!

Wine-Tasting Score Sheet

SCORE	DEFINITION
	SIGHT (0-4 points) Make sure you have a CLEAN narrow-mouthed wine glass. Fill the glass half-way, and hold it up against a white tablecloth, under white light. Is the color consistent from edge to edge? Is it murky? What are the bubbles like (if it's even supposed to have any!) When you pick up the glass, make sure you hold it by the stem. This keeps your hand from warming up the wine.
	SMELL (0-6 points) Close your eyes, swirl the wine around in the glass a bit to release the odors, and smell. What does the wine smell like? Berries? Leather? Tar? There will be smells both from the wine itself and also from whatever it was aged in. Does the smell start to alter as the wine warms up to room temperature?
	FLAVOR/TEXTURE (0-6 points) Pour some wine into your mouth and swirl it around a bit. Breathe out slowly through the nose to add smell into the taste (as you know, most of your 'taste' is actually smell). Is it greasy, or smooth? Is it mostly sour, or sweet? Are there new flavors you can sense now? The wine is warming in your mouth and might yet again change character. Swallow the wine, and see if there's any aftertaste.
	EVALUATION (0-4 points) How do you like the wine in general? Did it please you? What sticks most in your mind about this wine? Add comments below.
	TOTAL (0-20 points)

Dating Ideas

Stroll down the streets of Paris and you'll see couples in love. Walk along the beaches of the Mediterranean and it's love, love, love.

France is a country of love. Every thing you do can be romantic.

Here are a few ideas to get you started!

Music and Dance

Looking for fun ways to date in the French style? Go out to a night club! The French love spending the evening drinking and listening to fun music.

Experiment with what is local – find a guitarist one week, a blues singer the following week, a jazz pianist the third.

Expand your musical horizons and have fun seeing what sorts of people are attracted to each style of music.

People-Watching

Another classic tradition in France is to sit at a table outside a restaurant, where there are many people walking, and watch the people pass by. It's almost a national pastime.

Research your local area to see what open-air restaurants are available, and head out for a brunch or late-afternoon dinner.

Don't rush through the meal. Savor it. Watch in relaxation as life flows by around you.

Wine and Cheese

The French are quite enthusiastic about wine and cheese gatherings. Every day is a good day for a party!

Buy two bottles of French wine, get a selection of French cheese, and enjoy experimenting with them.

Which wine goes well with which cheese? Which do you prefer? You can easily make this into a weekly event with friends.

Painting Class

Have you seen those great offers where you pay once price and get to paint a painting, plus enjoy wine and food, with friends or loved ones? This is the way of the French! The French adore artwork – and they feel everyone should have a chance to try it. It's not just for the snooty, talented artists with years of training. Every person has creativity lurking within them.

Sign up for a night out. Have fun with it! Toast your friends and see what you can create together.

Courting

Voici mon secret. Il est très simple:
on ne voit bien qu'avec le coeur.
L'essentiel est invisible pour les yeux.

Here is my secret. It is very simple:
It is only with the heart that one can see rightly;
What is essential is invisible to the eye.
—The Little Prince, Antoine de Saint-Exupéry

The citizens of France felt that every day was a good day for courting, and any woman was to be gallantly flirted with. Love and romance was an everyday part of life, not something reserved for the young or for newlyweds.

Valentine's Day was a special day for extra outpourings of emotion. While most sweethearts would be sure to spend this day together, there were also traditions for the unattached. On the morning of St. Valentine's Day, the first man to be seen by a girl became her boyfriend or "valentine" for the day.

Flowers, always popular with the French, became even more closely linked with Valentine's Day when one of Henry IV's daughters received a bouquet from her chosen valentine. It is a tradition for flowers to be exchanged along with love notes, so feel free to shower your love with rhymes and roses!

A History of Dating in France

To love another person is to see the face of God.

—Les Miserables

In France, the rules of love and courtship had been set down in the 1100's, and men and women took this very seriously. Medieval singers in France spread songs with the ideals of love, and the songs and images echoed down through the ages. Men were to be gallant and charming, ready with a pleasing word for the women they met, no matter how high or low the female in station. Women were witty, alluring, and sensual. They would often find their best feature and would promote that charm to men. Their self-confidence and sensuality were more important than being born perfect. They did not need to be beautiful to be desirable.

Love and romance, sex and sensuality, these were all matters requiring practice, experience, and study. To the French, there were no quick tips, no easy shortcuts. Love and seduction were matters that were very important to respect, to control, to nurture with long, languorous touches.

The women of France were not necessarily beautiful. They examined themselves to learn how best to draw attention to their finest feature. They studied variations in fashion, trying different styles of hair, makeup, and clothing until they achieved the right effect. Sensuality to the French is about self-confidence and effect— to them, any woman can be alluring.

Courtship in France is referred to as "la drague." The woman does all the work preparing herself for the date, spending quite a bit of money on the right cosmetics, the right perfume, the perfect clothing to highlight her shape. The man then has to work very hard to show his worthiness. He holds open doors, waits on the woman, compliments her and flirts with her. He calls for more water at the restaurant and fetches her popcorn at the movies.

French men have a reputation for sweet-talking, and there is a reason for this. In the French culture, the man should make any woman within range of his voice feel that she is attractive, desirable, and worthy of attention. Doing this indicates that he is a gallant, caring male. The women then flirt back quite unabashedly, enjoying the attention. In general, the French are great flirts and enjoy the witty talk as good natured fun. Unlike other cultures where the men separate themselves from the women, in France, both genders mingle freely, enjoying the interplay.

By following the coy and flirtatious ways of the French, you can bring charm and romance to your sweetheart!

The Colors of Franc

The French flag is made up of the colors blue, white, and red. The French love colors and historical outfits were usually brightly colored. Families took pride in their heritage and would often wear colors found on their heraldry. Perhaps you can dress yourself and your home in the historic colors of your family!

Here are some of the more common French names and the colors associated with them:

Benoit: silver and blue

Bernard: silver and blue

Dubois: silver, red and gold

Durand: green, silver and gold

Gaillard: blue and gold

Laurent: red and silver

Martin: blue, black and silver

Moreau: silver and black

Petit: silver, black and red

Richard: blue, gold and silver

Riviere: blue and silver

Robert: blue, silver and gold

Flowers and Their Meanings

The little prince went away, to look again at the roses.

"You are not at all like my rose," he said. "As yet you are nothing. No one has tamed you, and you have tamed no one. You are like my fox when I first knew him. He was only a fox like a hundred thousand other foxes. But I have made him my friend, and now he is unique in all the world."

And the roses were very much embarrassed.

"You are beautiful, but you are empty," he went on. "One could not die for you. To be sure, an ordinary passerby would think that my rose looked just like you—the rose that belongs to me. But in herself alone she is more important than all the hundreds of you other roses: because it is she that I have watered; because it is she that I have put under the glass globe; because it is she that I have sheltered behind the screen; because it is for her that I have killed the caterpillars (except the two or three that we saved to become butterflies); because it is she that I have listened to, when she grumbled, or boasted, or even sometimes when she said nothing. Because she is my rose."

—The Little Prince

France is a land of vast flower-filled meadows and elegant gardens brimming with roses and orchids. No French village is complete without its overflowing window boxes and flower gardens. The hills of Provence explode with blossoms in the spring. Brides in France carried bouquets in their hands and wore wreaths of flowers in their hair. The church and reception hall fairly burst with floral arrangements.

Spring meant the arrival of colorful crocus bulbs, and gardeners could choose those representing their family colors. In the summer would come the tall purple lavender, the rich green ferns, and the colorful gladiolus. Other favorites in France include the iris, orchid, and poppy. Violets are famous for being the favorite flower of Josephine, wife of Napoleon. Perhaps flowers can bring a touch of romance to your life.

Here are the meanings of some of these flowers: crocus: cheerfulness, youth

gladiolus: beauty, strength

iris: promise

orchids: sensual, passionate poppies: memories

violet: love, true love

Roses were always a special flower to the French. From Romance of the Rose in the 1300s to the Little Prince's rose in the 1900s, roses were a symbol of the truest form of love. Here are some meanings of roses:

red rose: passionate love

white rose: innocence, purity

red and white roses together: unity, marriage

pink rose: appreciation, friendship

yellow rose: joy

rosebuds: youth, innocence

CDusic and Song

"No disguise can long conceal love where it exists, or long feign it where it is lacking."

—Francois La Rochefoucauld

French culture has always embraced music, especially songs that told stories. In medieval days, troubadours and knightly minstrels would travel the countryside, spreading tales of love and loss. In later years, music was an important part of any celebration.

Here is a love song from 1879, by Gabriel Faure

Notre amour et chose légère,	Our love is light and gentle,
Comme les parfums que le vent	Like the fragrance fetched by the breeze
Prend aux cimes de la fourère	From the tips of ferns
Pour qu'on les respire en rêvant.	For us to breathe while dreaming.
—Notre amour est chose légère.	—Our love is light and gentle.
Notre amour est chose charmante,	Our love is enchanting,
Comme les chanson du matin	Like morning songs,
Où nul regret ne se lamente,	Where no regret is voiced,
Où vibre un espoire incertain.	Quivering with uncertain hopes.
—Notre amour est chose charmante —	Our love is enchanting.
Notre amour est chose sacrée,	Our love is sacred,
Comme le mystère des bois	Like woodland mysteries,

Où tressaille une âme ignorée,

Où les silence ont des voix.

—Notre amour est chose sacrée.

Notre amour est chose infinie,

Comme les chemins des couchants

Où la mer, aux cieux réunie,

S'endort sous les soleils penchants.

—Notre amour est chose infinie,

Notre amour est chose éternelle,

Comme tout ce qu'un Dieu vainqueur

A touché du feu de son aile,

Comme tout ce qui vient due cœur,

—Notre amour est chose éternelle.

Where an unknown soul throbs,

And silences are eloquent.

—Our love is sacred.

Our love is infinite

Like sunset paths,

Where the sea, joined with the skies,

Falls asleep beneath slanting suns.

—Our love is infinite

Our love is eternal,

Like all that a victorious God

Has brushed with his fiery wing,

Like all that comes from the heart,

—Our love is eternal.

Love Poetry

France has a long tradition of love poetry. The ideal love was not arranged or forced, it was gently urged and persuaded. There are many, many poems in France's history that talk about love, and its importance to both man and woman.

The Romance of the Rose

The first tales of courtly love were created in France under Eleanor of Aquitaine's rule. In the 1200s, Guillaume de Lorris and Jean de Meun wrote The Romance of the Rose, an allegorical poem about love. It is made up of over 20,000 lines and took over forty years to complete. It talks of a rose kept safe in a garden, whose beauty is overpowering and pleasing, and uses allegories of danger, mirth, and pleasure.

Woman should gather roses 'ere

Time's ceaseless foot o'ertaketh her,

For if too long she make delay,

Her chance of love may pass away,

And well it is she seek it while

Health, strength, and youth around her smile.

To pluck the fruits of love in youth

Is each wise woman's rule forsooth,

For when age creepeth o'er us, hence So also the sweet joys of sense,

And ill doth she her days employ

Who lets life pass without love's joy.

And if my counsel she despise,

Not knowing how 'tis just and wise,

Too late, alas! will she repent

When age is come, and beauty spent.

Alphonse De LaMartine

In the late 1700s, Alphonse de Lamartine penned his verse. Some famous quotes include:

"To love for the sake of being loved is human; but to love for the sake of loving is angelic."

and

"There is a woman at the beginning of all great things."

Here is a beautifully evocative poem about youth and love:

Butterfly

To be born with the spring, and with the roses die,

On the wing of the breeze swim through the sky so pure, Balanced on the breast of flowers barely closed, Drinking in their perfumes, the light and the blue sky, Shaking off, still so young, the dust upon its wings, Flying off like a breath to the eternal vault,

This is the butterfly's enchanted destiny! It's like the desire that is never addressed,

And left unsatisfied, should it brush against anything, Returns in the end to the sky, seeking its sensual pleasure.

Victor Hugo

Writing later in the 1800s was Victor Hugo, famous for his masterpiece Les Miserables. It is from that book that the quote "To love another person is to see the face of God" comes. In addition to his fine plays and poetry, he was also an artist and journalist. He was well respected during his time for his many talents, and his works have a timeless appeal. Here are two of his love poems.

Oh, Why Not Be Happy

Oh, why not be happy this bright summer day 'Mid perfume of roses and newly mown hay? Great Nature is smiling, the birds in the air Sing love-lays together, and all is most fair.

Then why not be happy This bright summer day

'Mid perfume of roses And newly mown hay ?

The streamlets they wander through meadows so fleet,

Their music enticing fond lovers to meet;

The violets are blooming and nestling their heads

In richest profusion on moss-coated beds.

Then why not be happy This bright summer day

When Nature is fairest and all is so gay?

If My Verses Had the Wings

Songs as sweet as summer brings,

To your flowery lawn should fly

If my verses had the wings—

Wings of birds that haunt the sky.

Like the spark that upward springs,

They would seek your smiling hearth,

If my verses had the wings—

Wings such as a spirth hath.

Near you, close as ivy clings,

They would dwell by night and day

If my verses had the wings—

Wings like love to speed the way.

Antoine de Saint Exupery

A more modern French poet was Antoine de Saint Exupery (1900—1944). His airplane was shot down during WWII, but before that he wrote many famous poems and books, including *The Little Prince*. Some sources state that *The Little Prince* is the third most-read book of the 20th century.

One of the core themes of *The Little Prince* is the Prince's undying love for a beautiful rose which he picked from among hundreds of other roses, and cared for tenderly.

"If some one loves a flower, of which just one single blossom grows in all the millions and millions of stars, it is enough to make him happy just to look at the stars. He can say to himself, 'Somewhere, my flower is there...'"

The beauty of *The Little Prince* rests in the way it takes the ordinary – a fox, a boy, a rose – and brings their relationship into the realm of the extraordinary. By simple analogy, the characters bring us face to face with our fondest hopes and wishes, and the human striving to love and to be loved.

By the way, this is a lovely story to read aloud to your sweetheart.

Words and Phrases

French is often called the 'language of love' because it flows so smoothly from the tongue. Practice a few French words and phrases and wonder at their beauty! Certainly, a marriage proposal in the language of romance can hardly be denied!

beautiful: beau

marriage: mariage

darling: chéri

marry: mariez

happy: hereaux

sweetheart: amoureux

husband: mari wife: épouse

love: amour

I love you: je t'aime

Will you marry me: volonté tu m'épousez

Choosing a Mate

While the French are very religious, and marriages to bring together families were common in years past, the French traditions of passionate love bringing a couple together are very powerful. The French today choose their mates with passion, and ask their hand in marriage with panache!

Read on to learn more about taking romance to the next level.

Traditions of Matchmaking

In the middle ages in France, property was a primary concern in match-making. It was such a high priority that there were two types of legal marriage. The first was Muntehe, where property changed hands from the father of the bride to the bride's new husband. The second was Friedelehe, which was also a legal marriage, but in this case property did not change hands. For example, Charlemagne only allowed his daughters to Friedelehe marry their loved ones, so that he retained full control over his lands.

Even through the renaissance, young adults would be expected to follow their parents' instructions on who to marry, as it would have a great impact on family fortunes and standing. Still, as the decades passed, the draw of love and romance caused more and more marriages to be based on true love and desire.

Where other cultures would divine about husbands with sticks and nuts, the French believed firmly in the power of the Virgin Mary over such things. Young girls and women would pray nightly to the Virgin Mary, hoping for a husband who was caring and honest. The popularity of the Virgin Mary was increased greatly after a sighting in La Salette on September 19, 1846 by two shepherd children. A subsequent sighting in Lourdes ensured the Virgin Mary's continued popularity in France.

The Proposal

The French cherished a culture of love and romance, and a year or more of courtship and wooing was expected before a man asked for a woman's hand in marriage. A classic saying about marriage was:

Qui se marie à la hâte se repent à loisir.

Meaning,

"Marry in haste, repent at leisure."

The suitor would usually ask the father for permission first and work out the arrangements of the dowry he was to receive. He would present his own rank, status, and earning potential so he might be deemed worthy.

The actual proposal would be a formal act and would involve the exchanging of rings. In addition, there was usually a toast of wine, and sometimes the sharing of a piece of fruit to seal the arrangement.

The relationship is taken quite seriously. A public (Facebook-style) announcement would never be made until all close family and friends had been personally notified.

Engagement Rings

One of the signs of true love in France is the posy ring. Interestingly, this ring has nothing to do with flowers. Posy comes from the French word for "poetry," and referred to the sentiment behind the ring. Often the words "Pensez de Moy"—old French for "think of me" - would be inscribed inside the ring. Words on the inside were felt to have more power, as they touched the skin of the wearer and remained secret from the world.

A posy ring was worn on the third (ring) finger, as it was believed that the vein in this finger ran straight to the heart. Here are some common ring inscriptions:

nul autre—no other

ma vie et mon amour—my life and my love

l'amour nous unit—love unites us

mon amour est infini—my love is endless

sans de partir—never to part

mon coeur aves—you have my heart

For most of France's history, an engagement ring would be a posy band of gold, perhaps with a gem that was meaningful to the couple. It might be her birthstone, or his birthstone, or maybe a color in one of their family's crests. The emerald was especially linked to sexual passion and love.

King Louis IX of France had forbidden diamonds to be worn by any but the king. Not even his Queen or daughters could wear diamonds. When King Charles VII of France gave his mistress diamonds to wear in the mid-1400s, the sparkling gems became a definitive symbol of romance. The edict against diamond wearing was fully broken when Emperor Maximilian I took as a bride Mary of Burgundy in 1477, giving her a stunning diamond engagement ring.

In modern times, the bride-to-be often gives the groom an expensive watch, rather than an engagement ring of his own to wear.

Ring Finger

It's interesting to think that modern couples always put the engagement ring on the third (ring) finger of the hand. This is the finger directly next to the smallest pinkie finger. Some cultures use the left hand for romantic rings, while other cultures used the right hand.

In the Middle Ages and the renaissance, this third finger was chosen because they felt the vein in this finger was the 'vein of love' and led directly to the heart. Before that, most rings were placed on the index (first) finger, perhaps because this was the strongest finger and showed the most powerful emotion.

The Bridal Trousseau

A hope chest is a tradition in many modern families. It is a wooden trunk, often built by hand by a family member, given to a female child at her birth. As she grows up, gifts are given to the girl for her to use when she becomes older and marries.

This tradition originated in France with the "trousseau." The word literally means "little bundle," and referred to the clothing and personal items that a new bride would carry along with her to her new home. Parents would often set aside a drawer or small box for the girl to store special items in, to keep them clean until her wedding day.

As time went on, the bridal chest became more and more elaborate. The chest became a status symbol for the bride, both for its fine construction as well as the costly items it would hold. The more wealthy brides would have an extremely expensive chest, created with fine woods and inlays, and containing silver cutlery, linens, and other household items.

Engagement Traditions

With the French wedding being a combination of an extremely important religious ceremony, a legally binding merger of two families, and a love match between two enthusiastic individuals, it is no surprise that wedding preparations could take on mammoth proportions. Everything from the paper for the invitation to the color of the flowers would be planned, scrutinized and discussed for months.

Everything from the family's colors to the favorite picnic locations of the couple would be taken into account as the plans moved forward. If you are involved in the planning of a wedding, give yourself plenty of time to consider just about every angle! It could be that some small detail about the restaurant the couple first ate in, or the flowers she first received, could be a perfect theme for the wedding.

Choosing a Wedding Date

While in neighboring Italy a wedding was supposed to be held on Sunday to emphasize the religious significance of the match, in France and other European countries it was practically forbidden to have such celebration on a holy day. Instead, French weddings were scheduled mid-week, so that the new couple would be fully settled before the next Sunday rolled around and they were expected to attend church for the first time as a married couple.

The traditional rhyme goes:

Monday for wealth

Tuesday for health

Wednesday the best day of all

Thursday for losses

Friday for crosses

Saturday for no luck at all

Sunday was not even included in the rhyme, as it was not under consideration.

Couples were advised not to marry in the month of May or in the fall. One reason was that these were traditional planting and harvesting times, and the attention of the couple and family should be on doing these activities. Also, May was both the month of pagan fertility rites and the month dedicated to the Virgin Mary. On one hand, the marriage should be quite separate from the wildness of the rites, and on the other hand, the Virgin Mary's month should be dedicated to her alone and not to other celebrations.

The Invitation

The French are famous for their literature and fine printing. They treasure the fine parchment that books are written on, the choice of font, the decorative touches. Many famous love stories have been written by French authors over the centuries, and those books held respected positions on many shelves.

A French wedding invitation is therefore created to be a thing of beauty, something that will last for years and be treasured. To start with, it would be created on fine paper, something which would stand the test of time. Its quality would reflect the quality of the individuals who were to be wed.

If the couple can afford it, hand calligraphy would be the ultimate statement of care – that each invitation was created especially for that person. It again adds to the meaning of the invitation. If this would be cost-prohibitive, there are many fonts which imitate calligraphy that could be used.

The French are very fond of decorative touches, so many invitations would include fine scrollwork on the borders. For a traditional touch of French design, you can add in a fleur de lis -

Family was extremely important to the French, and family symbols and colors were often used in a wedding. If you are of French descent and have researched your family coat of arms, include it to symbolize that it is two families, and not just two individuals, who will be joined.

While we're talking about the invitation, did you know that RSVP stands for répondez s'il vous plaît - which means "respond, please." It's a phrase found on most wedding invitations!

The Fiançailles

The Fiançailles are the engagement dinner that helps to blend the two families together into one hopefully harmonious whole. It's a day – or series of days – where the parents and siblings can scope each other out and get to know each other.

French relationships are strong on family ties. There is an expectation that the families will blend into one larger unit.

French Wedding Blessings

The French had many blessings, poems and sayings about love.
Here are some classic sayings that you might use in your invitations.

Joan of Arc prayer:

*O God, by whom the meek are guided in judgment, and light riseth
up in darkness for the godly: grant us, in all our doubts and
uncertainties, to ask what thou wouldst have us to do; that the
spirit of wisdom may save us from all false choices, that in thy light
we may see light, and in thy straight paths may not stumble, this
which we ask through Jesus Christ our Lord, who liveth and
reigneth with thee and the Holy Spirit, one God, for ever and ever.*

The Virgin Mary is especially important to young women and brides,
and often she is specially honored during a French wedding
ceremony. This can take many forms. Some French brides would
have 'Ave Maria' sung as people were seated, or even as the bride
walked down the aisle to her husband-to-be.

One prayer which works well for a wedding is Our Lady of the
Sacred Heart:

*Remember, Our Lady of the Sacred Heart, what ineffable power thy
divine Son hath given thee over His own adorable Heart. Full of
trust in thy merits, we come before thee and beg thy protection. O
heavenly Treasurer of the Heart of Jesus, that Heart which is the
inexhaustible source of all graces, which thou mayest open to us at
thy good pleasure, in order that from it may flow forth upon
mankind the riches of love and mercy, light and salvation, that
are contained therein; grant unto us, we beseech thee, the favors
which we seek . . . We can never, never be refused by thee, and since
thou art our Mother, O our Lady of the Sacred Heart, graciously
hear our prayers and grant our request. Amen.*

One of the most famous wedding blessings is used very frequently in
French weddings.

1 Corinthians 13

If I speak in the tongues of men and of angels, but have not love, I am only a resounding gong or a clanging cymbal.

If I have the gift of prophecy and can fathom all mysteries and all knowledge, and if I have a faith that can move mountains, but have not love, I am nothing.

If I give all I possess to the poor and surrender my body to the flames, but have not love, I gain nothing.

Love is patient, love is kind. It does not envy, it does not boast, it is not proud.

It is not rude, it is not self-seeking, it is not easily angered, it keeps no record of wrongs.

Love does not delight in evil but rejoices with the truth.

It always protects, always trusts, always hopes, always perseveres.

Love never fails. But where there are prophecies, they will cease; where there are tongues, they will be stilled; where there is knowledge, it will pass away.

For we know in part and we prophesy in part, but when perfection comes, the imperfect disappears.

When I was a child, I talked like a child, I thought like a child, I reasoned like a child. When I became a man, I put childish ways behind me.

Now we see but a poor reflection as in a mirror; then we shall see face to face. Now I know in part; then I shall know fully, even as I am fully known.

And now these three remain: faith, hope and love. But the greatest of these is love.

Note that if your wedding is a Roman Catholic one, you can get an official blessing from the Pope, to frame and hang on your wall. You'll need to speak with the Chancellor or Chancery office of your Diocese to get the appropriate forms, and it can take up to six months to process.

Well worth the wait, this can be a truly special way to celebrate your special day for the rest of your lives.

Sayings about Marriage

The pragmatists in France often viewed marriage as a necessity, and love as a special treat that might accompany a marriage. One traditional saying about marriage is:

"Love is often the fruit of marriage"

Another marriage saying is:

"A happy marriage is a long conversation which always seems too short."

—Andre Maurois, French writer

One saying which shows how much the French valued rank and status is:

"A good name is better than riches."

—Bonne renommée vaut mieux que ceinture dorée.

The French realized that life isn't smooth, but that challenges are shared in a marriage. Still, they enjoy emphasizing that this is just a part of life, one that can be worked through.

Every country has its share of bad roads.

En tout pays, il y a une lieue de mauvais chemin.

The French believe that true love exists for every human, no matter how unlikely. This sentiment is portrayed in many stories and folklore. No matter what a person looks like or the amount of money they have, there will always someone out there that will be a perfect partner. There is always the potential for true happiness.

Presents

While other cultures might focus on registries and the bride getting to choose in exact detail what they will get, France isn't quite like this. They tend not to go in for a bride making a giant wish-list of what she wants.

Instead, everyone gives the couple cash. That way the couple can recoup the expense they just went through to throw a massive party and then enjoy a luxurious honeymoon afterwards!

On the other hand, the bride and groom often take great delight in hand-making all the favors for the guests. Whether it's homemade wine or hand-canned jam, the couple ensures that the family and friends who share in the party get something that is truly personal and special to take home with them.

The Night Before

For the French in bygone days, the wedding was a formal, religious ceremony the union of two families, often involving a transfer of land. The night before therefore was a time for each family to share one last meal together, to pray for health and happiness, to rest and prepare for the day to come.

A tradition for the woman was to have a long ritual bath.

This was, of course, extremely soothing to the body and the mind. It represented a final purification for the woman, to wash away from her any evil thoughts and acts from her past. It was also supposed to cleanse her of any thoughts of any other man.

Rosewater was the optimal choice for bathing, for it not only cleansed the mind and soul, but also brought forth thoughts of love and passion for the new husband to be.

The Wedding

A wedding day in France traditionally came after a long period of courting and a long engagement. Every preparation was made for this day, in hopes that all would be perfect. It was a religious ceremony, binding a couple together with an oath before God.

Often it was also a solemn transfer of land and wealth from one family to another. Perhaps most importantly, it involved the ranks and statuses of both families, and it was very important to both that this change in status be recognized and celebrated by the entire village. And, last but not least, it was a new beginning, as man and woman stepped forward to become husband and wife.

Gecting To the Church

In some cultures, the bride was hidden away on the wedding day, even veiled, so that the groom only saw her in the church and only saw her face after the wedding. That traces to the old tradition of arranged marriages, to try to prevent the groom from changing his mind should his bride lack beauty. The French take the exact opposite approach. By having a long courtship and engagement, they make sure that the bride and groom are fully happy with the arrangement before the wedding day comes along. And, on the wedding day, the groom proudly arrives at the house of the bride to escort her and her family to the church.

The village church was usually within walking distance of the bride's home, and the procession would be accompanied by musicians strolling alongside. The bride would walk with her father, and the groom with his mother, while the rest of the family came along with them. This symbolized the joining of the two families, not just the two individuals.

The local villagers would join in the fun of this parade. They would place various obstacles in front of the couple, which they needed to overcome to show their determination to marry. Ribbons might be draped across the street and the bride and groom would need to cut them to go past. Sometimes briars would be placed in their path, to show that marriage was not always easy, and the couple would diligently work through the briars.

When the group reached the church, the groom would escort his mother to her seat. This shows that he is with the two women he loves the most – his mother and his bride to be. He would then wait at the front of the church while the bride's father escorted the bride to join him at the altar.

The bride would walk on a path of laurel leaves, to celebrate her arrival at the ceremony.

The Groom

In the days of chivalry, a French knight would wear a token of his lady's affection into battle. This token was a personal item of hers, often a handkerchief she had embroidered, bearing her family colors. The knight would wear the token for luck, and to show that he fought bravely in order to honor her.

The flower of the groom taken from the bouquet of the bride conveys the same meaning. The groom is publicly wearing a token from his love. The name "boutonniere" for this flower is, of course, French.

If the man was a soldier, he would wear his uniform. Otherwise, he would wear his best clothing. A man would rarely buy a special suit just for this one day.

Wedding Dress

In the medieval days, and even early renaissance days of France, most people could not afford special clothing. The best dress the woman owned would become her wedding dress. This dress was then embroidered and worked on with lace, tassels, and ribbons, to make it truly special. Think of the scene in Disney's "Cinderella", where Cinderella valiantly works to make one of her dresses magnificent for the ball.

A wedding dress was certainly not white – white was reserved for mourning royalty. The dress chosen would normally be in the family colors of the bride, to show that her family was joining with another. If a color was chosen other than the family color, it would be blue, for this was the traditional color of purity.

The traditional color was first challenged by Ann of Brittany. When she married Louis XII of France in the early 1500's, she wore white. The white dress tradition was continued by Mary, Queen of Scots, when she married the Dauphin in France in 1558. As time went on, silver and white parties became very fashionable, and the French nobles would throw lavish balls with all white dress. There is a celebration of this type shown in the Michael York version of the Three Musketeers, near the end of the film.

Still, white dresses did not become a tradition for most people in France until the 1800's. This was primarily due to cost – most families simply could not afford to buy a special dress for this one occasion.

The French loved flowers, and the bride would usually wear a wreath of flowers in her hair. The flowers would usually be roses, the flowers of love. Other flowers were often woven in as well.

In modern times French brides will often go for the "something old, something new, something borrowed, something blue" – a tradition they borrowed from the English.

Bridesmaids and Groomsmen

When you look at wedding portraits, you often see that the men all dress very similarly to one another, as do the women. This comes from an ancient Roman tradition. Evil spirits were thought to be jealous of the love of the bride and groom, and would wish to cause trouble for them. The bridesmaids and groomsmen would dress similarly to confuse these spirits, and foil their attempts.

But, this being said, in modern times the French tend to simply have "witnesses." The men will wear suits, and the women will wear pretty dresses. They don't tend to be as perfectly matched as you would find in an American wedding.

Church Decorations

In medieval days, the French would fill the church with flowers and incense, beautifying the sanctuary. This was also practical in a day when people did not bathe often – the extra-long ceremony might be a bit difficult to tolerate with so many in a space so close!

The pews, altar and hallways would be lavishly decorated with flowers, echoing the colors chosen by the bride. There would be a large floral arch at the entry to the main hall, and flowers on the stairs leading from the church.

Often a special bouquet would be laid by a statue of the Virgin Mary, to honor her during this ceremony. In some French weddings, the bride would stop at the statue either on her way to or from the altar, and take a flower from her own bouquet to lay by the statue in thanks.

White and red roses were both popular colors for a bouquet or head wreath.

Orange blossoms were also traditionally included at weddings as a symbol of a happy marriage. This originated with a French ambassador to Spain, who desperately wanted an orange tree. At the time, Spanish gardeners were protecting their trees fiercely. The French ambassador talked a gardener's daughter into getting him a clipping. In return, he provided her with a large dowry so that she was able to marry the man she loved. In thanks to him for making her dreams come true, the Spanish bride wore orange blossoms in her hair when she married.

The French Ceremony

The French ceremony would be a full mass, with the marriage vows included. The French were extremely religious people and would make sure that this ceremony was one of great respect.

The couple would stand together at the altar underneath a "carre," or silk canopy. This would shield the pair from any evil influences that might disrupt their happiness. Often, this silk fabric was then saved to be used at their childrens' baptisms.

In some areas of France, while the ceremony was proceeding, the groom would rest his foot on the bride's shoe, to keep her from running off, and to show his authority over her during her transition from the child of her father to his wife.

It's important to note that in modern times couples get both a religious and a civil ceremony. So the celebration often goes on for the entire weekend!

After the Ceremony

A floral arch often decorated the entryway of the church, and the new couple walked through it on their way out into the village square. They were showered with various symbols of fertility–rice, wheat, seeds, or even bread. Some areas also added tokens of wealth, often small coins. Laurel leaves, a symbol of success, were scattered at the couple's feet to congratulate them.

If you're fond of the rice tradition, you need not worry as many do about how it will affect birds that eat the rice. Birds' stomachs do not explode when they eat rice, as some people fear. You can join in this French tradition assured that you will not harm your feathered friends!

Another traditional item to toss was the dragées. Dragées are almonds coated in chocolate, which symbolize that marriage is at once both bitter and sweet.

Church bells would peal loudly, to announce the wedding to all within earshot, and to drive away any evil spirits which might still linger nearby.

There are tales of weddings in the 1500's, where the new man and wife would strip naked outside the church door, and the groom would kiss the feet of his wife, promising to take good care of her. Luckily, this custom did not remain popular for very long!

The Reception

The French love food, wine, and music, and a wedding reception is the perfect time for all three. While the ceremony is a formal vow before God and a legal joining of two families, the reception is a chance for everyone to relax, have fun, and celebrate the success of the arrangement. The wedding reception was usually held at the home of the bride or groom's parents, wherever was most convenient and properly sized.

The following sections help you plan your own reception so you can celebrate with the sprit, or *esprit*, of France.

Traditions for a Happy Marriage

One of the traditional presents for a new French couple was the wedding quilt. The quilt was often created by relatives working together in secret while the wedding was being planned. The quilt would be made all in white, with the new couple's initials and date of marriage. It would often have symbols of fertility, love, prosperity, and long life sewn into it.

Other traditional wedding presents include flowers and fruit, to bring beauty and delicious flavor to the new couple's life together.

The couple would also give gifts to their bridesmaids and groomsmen in thanks for their help. Bridesmaids would often receive elegant fans, often with images of lovers or romance painted on them. Men would often receive bottles of wine.

The Garter

Called "la jarretière" in French, the garter is a regular piece of lingerie that women wore to hold up their stockings. In the days before elastic, the garter kept the stockings from slipping down.

The bride was considered to be very lucky on her wedding day, and any piece of clothing she wore was thought to be equally lucky. Her dress was her best outfit and would not be taken, but anything else she wore was sought after by revelers to bring some of the bride's luck to them.

In the medieval days, the best man would try to 'steal' the garter from the bride, and then sell pieces of it to the guests to share in the bride's fertility and make money to pay the musicians. As weddings got more and more raucous, and guests became a little too eager to get their share of the fertility luck, and would make attempts for the garter themselves. To protect his bride, the groom removed the garter himself and then it flung the item to the crowd.

This same desire to share in the bride's luck also affected anything she carried. Her flowers were thought to be extremely potent in luck and love. To maintain some order to the celebration, the bride soon took to tossing her bride's bouquet at an announced time to whoever would wish to catch it.

Indeed, anything worn by or carried by the bride was considered to bring fertility and luck to whoever acquired it.

Decorations and Flowers

Just as the church was full of flowers and fragrance, so was the reception hall bedecked and adorned. In fact, villagers would often bring additional flowers with them, to help decorate the rooms. Roses were commonly chosen for this task, but violets and others flowers would often be used as well.

Common floral themes would include the colors of the families who were being joined together, as well as white for innocence, blue for purity, and red for love.

Music and Dance

There are several ways to bring a French touch to the music at a wedding reception. For an elegant reception or to accompany the cocktail portion of a dinner, you might hire a classical quartet to play period music. Claude Debussy (1862-1918) was a French composer who wrote beautiful music, including his Nocturnes and Etudes. Maurice Ravel is another French composer you might feature during the evening. Both of these men created mellifluous music that makes a perfect accompaniment to such festivities.

For the post-dinner party, there are many French folk songs you can use that are quite popular. To go with a WWII theme, you can choose French dance tunes from the 1940s and 1950s. Those would prove quite an attraction for any guests you have that are fond of that era.

The French tradition does not include any well-known wedding dances like the Italian Tarantella. The French people simple love to dance, and just about any music you play will find an audience for dancing. At a French wedding, happiness is in the air. The revelers talk, have fun, and enjoy the music and food!

French parties often begin to pick up steam about midnight – and are often going well into the dawn hours again.

Also note that modern French weddings often involve an "embarrass the couple" stage, where silly photos and videos are shown of the couple when they were young, foolish, or both. It can get quite wild!

A French Wedding Cake

During the middle ages, guests would all bring spiced cakes as a treat to the wedding. In essence, the entire village would bake to help celebrate the marriage. The cakes would all be piled together, and then the bride and groom would have to see if they could kiss over the top of it.

When King Charles II married, the mound was so huge that the chefs added icing to stick it together, so that it wouldn't fall over. Thus was born the single wedding cake. The French, with their love of beauty, brought the wedding cake to the level of artistry that we enjoy today.

If you're interested in a traditional French wedding cake, these confections were celebrations of fancy ingredients and exotic flavors. The wedding was a chance to try a special treat that was not normally affordable. Here is a recipe from the renaissance, a rich, resplendent cake with a sweet and succulent flavor.

Traditional French Wedding Cake Recipe

1 lb powdered sugar
1 lb butter
10 eggs
2 tsp allspice
1 tsp cinnamon
1 tsp cloves
1 tsp nutmeg
tsp mace
¼ cup molasses
1 lb flour, sifted
2 lb currants
lb raisins
½ cup rum
½ cup brandy

First blend together the sugar and butter. Add in the eggs and blend well. In a separate bowl, mix together the allspice, cinnamon, cloves, nutmeg, and mace. Mix this in to the butter mixture.

Stir in the molasses, then the flour. Now add in the raisins, rum, and brandy. Mix well. Grease and flour a 9" x 13" pan, and cook at 200°F for 5 hours. Cool for at least another 5 hours before icing.

The Wedding Toast

The French love their wine and liqueur, so it is no surprise that many say the wedding toast originated in France. A piece of bread would be put in the bottom of two drinking glasses, and each would be filled with wine. One would be given to the bride, and one to the groom. The two would both drink as quickly as they could to reach the toast first. Whoever did was said to be the ruler of the household!

The traditional French toast is "A votre santé", or "to your health." With wine now a recommended part of a healthy diet, the French were quite wise to say this!

Another French wine tradition emphasized the joining of the families. Each couple would pour a glass of their favorite wine from a vineyard local to their family. The two would then pour both wines into a third glass, blending the wines, and share this glass together.

The "Coupe de Marriage", or marriage cup, was a two-handled large toasting cup. This large cup was designed for the two lovers to drink from together. This coupe was often a very finely wrought goblet, and would be passed down from generation to generation within a family.

Note that traditionally, a person being toasted is not supposed to drink. The person is supposed to be grateful to the toasters, and give thanks for the honor. The honored person can then propose a new toast, and partake in the drinking of that one.

Fun Champagne Toasts

With Champagne hailing from France, be sure to toast early and often during your reception!

Friendship's the wine of life. Let's drink of it and to it.

Here's Champagne to our real friends

and real pain to our sham friends.

Some friends wish you happiness, and others with you wealth.

But I wish you the best of all contentment blessed with health!

May you have warm words on a cold evening,

a full moon on a dark night,

and the road downhill all the way to your door.

There are good ships and there are wood ships

the ships that sail the sea but the best ships

are friendships

and may they always be.

May your troubles be less and your blessings be more

and nothing but happiness come through the door.

Accept that some days you're the pigeon

And some days you're the statue.

To eternity, may it last forever!

May you live as long as you want to,

and may you want to as long as you live!

Clinking of Wine Glasses and Toasts

As with many of our food traditions, the clinking of glasses traces its root to the health and safety of the drinker. In this case, it goes back to the tendency of nobles to kill each other off by poisoning their food!

Wine was very commonly drunk during medieval days because it was one of the only safe liquids available. Water was often polluted, and milk was both useful for other things and thought to be for children only. As the wine was often full of sediment, a poison was easily introduced into it.

To prove that his wine was safe, the host would pour a bit of his guest's wine into his own glass and drink it first, to prove it was safe. If the guest trusted his host, however, he would merely clink his flagon against that of his host's when his host offered his cup for the sample. The 'clink' (or perhaps 'clunk' back then, since wood or metal was more common for drinking vessels) was a sign of trust and honesty.

Later, as metal and glass became more common, the chiming noise also brought a festive feel to events, and brought to mind the 'safe' feeling of church bells.

So clink your glass with each toast. Celebrate your love and trust!

how to Open Champagne

Bubbly is always expected during a celebration. French Champagne is the world-renowned standard, and has been used in celebrations since the 1800s.

Here is a step-by-step guide on how to properly open a bottle of Champagne. Remember, your primary goal in opening a bottle of Champagne is to control the cork and, of course, not to let much of the drink spill.

Every bottle of Champagne or sparkling wine (with a few low-end exceptions) has foil wrapped around the outside of the cork. In the old days, some foil was lead-lined to keep mice from eating into the cork, but this is no longer the case.

From this point onward, keep the cork pointed in a safe direction, and keep one thumb on it, just in case. Corks can loosen over time, so even if you think you're not ready to pop the cork yet, the bottle may have a different idea.

Untwist and remove the wire cage. This cage ensures that the cork does not pop out of the bottle until you are ready to have it do so. Loosen it gently, being sure to keep a thumb on the cork to prevent it from flying out prematurely.

Most people put a towel over the cork at this point, to help control the cork's exit from the bottle.

Hold the cork in one hand (usually under a towel), and the base of the bottle in the other. Turn the Bottle, not the cork, slowly and gently. You want the cork to ease off with a soft "whoof", not with a loud pop.

By gently removing the cork, you have saved the bubbles and air from being immediately lost (never mind the Champagne!). Still, with the pressure removed, you should now quickly pour it out for consumption. Slide the towel around to the neck of the bottle for pouring.

You will find that a quick turn of the bottle when you're done pouring each glass will catch the drops on the edge of the lip. Pour the Champagne down the sides of the glasses to minimize foam and therefore bubble waste.

The glasses are poured! Raise them, and give a toast to celebrate!

By the way, never use a corkscrew on a bottle of Champagne! The bottle is under strong pressure and could explode.

The French love their Champagne, and they enjoy drinking it mixed with other beverages as well as by itself.

Mimosa

Ingredients:

Orange Juice

Champagne

Serve in a Champagne saucer or flute. Fill the glass about 1/4 with orange juice. Fill the rest with chilled Champagne. Garnish with a round slice of orange.

You can also add in orange liqueur for an added kick!

Kir Royale

Ingredients:

3/4 oz. Creme de Cassis

Champagne

Pour the Creme de Cassis in the bottom of a wine glass or Champagne flute. Fill the glass the rest of the way with Champagne. Garnish with a twist of lemon.

French 75

Ingredients:

1 oz Sour mix

1 oz Cognac

Chilled Champagne

Stir the sour mix and the Cognac in a collins glass with just a bit of ice. Fill the glass with Champagne. Garnish with a French flag.

Chartreuse

The history of this French liqueur dates back to 1605, in Vauvert, near Paris. It was in this year that the Carthusian monks were given a copy of a recipe for the "Elixir of Long Life." This potent recipe called for a base of 70% wine alcohol, plus 130 herbs and spices. By the 1700's the monks were creating a medicinal elixir based on this recipe.

In the 1800s they had created Green Chartreuse—at 55% alcohol— and Yellow Chartreuse—at a mild 40%. Green Chartreuse is the more flavorful of the two, while the yellow is a bit minty and sweeter.

Although they strived to keep the recipe a secret, Napoleon gained possession of the recipe for a short while. Fortunately, he found it too difficult to make correctly. As the fame of Chartreuse spread, even foreign tsars demanded Chartreuse be served at state functions. The French government, jealous of the liqueur's popularity, nationalized the monastery. The monks fled to Spain with the recipe, and despite the best attempts of the French government, they were unable to discover how to make the drink.

The monks have since returned to the monastery. Three monks are the sole holders of the secret recipe, and it is due to the monastery's efforts that the rest of the world enjoys this fine liqueur.

Champagne & Cheese

Champagne and Cheese is a classic combination. You don't normally want to eat a whole meal with Champagne—you want to savor the fine wine and enjoy its texture and flavor. Cheese is a good thing to nibble at while you do so—to complement the flavor.

Brie
Brie is a soft, creamy French cheese that is best served very fresh. This goes wonderfully with a gentle Champagne, something light and fruity.

Mild cheddar
Cheddar is an English cheese that most people have tried at some point. The French and the English may not get along all too well, but the cheeses certainly do! Choose a mild, young cheddar; it will go well with some of the sharper, brighter Champagnes.

Chevre
How appropriate! Chevre is the French word for "goat cheese." Make sure it's fresh, and it will have a mild but tangy flavor to it. Use this with the stronger Champagnes that have a bit of kick to them.

Colby
Colby is a hard, mild cheese often associated with Port. It's originally from Wisconsin, and does go very well with Champagne as well. Try this with a medium-bodied Champagne.

Edam
Edam is a semi-hard, creamy cheese from Holland. It's slightly nutty, so it's a great pairing with the many Champagnes that have that nutty undertone to them.

Gouda
Gouda is another Dutch cheese, this one hard and smooth. As it also has a nutty flavor to it, it also pairs wonderfully with the nutty Champagnes.

Champagne & Appetizers

There are classic combinations that are truly delicious. The key is to remember that Champagne is light and delicate – find a light, airy appetizer to match.

Fois Gras
Yes, liver. Champagne is traditionally paired with duck or goose liver. The soft, smooth texture of the fois gras pairs nicely with the gentle bubbles and delicate flavor of Champagne.

Raw Oysters
Avoid the lemon or vinegar when you're serving these with Champagne.

Raw Shrimp
A raw shrimp appetizer is a perfect pairing with Champagne. Just avoid that heavy red sauce.

Stuffed Mushrooms
Mushrooms and Champagne are a great pairing, so any sort of appetizer you can create using mushrooms will go quite nicely.

Sushi
I love sushi, and Champagne goes perfectly with it. At your next party, put out some sushi appetizers with the Champagne and watch the smiles begin!

Champagne & Desserts

If you're planning a dessert tray for your reception, be sure to include treats that go nicely with Champagne!

Strawberries
This is a classic for romantic occasions, but it only works with very sweet sparklers! Try this with Pommery Pop, in the small blue bottles. All you need are a pair of flutes to clink, and a serving of strawberries to savor by hand. You might even feed each other one or two.

Tarts & Crumbles
Fruit dishes that are fresh and light work perfectly well—an apple tart, a pear crumble.

Fruit Puddings
Another great dish with Champagne is plum pudding or rice pudding. This is perfect for holiday celebrations! Again, if you use a sweeter pudding, be sure to pair it with a sweeter Champagne.

Shortbread and Almond Cookies
Choose light, delicate cookies to match well with Champagne's bubbles and freshness. Kugelhopf is a classic almond cake that does quite nicely.

FRENCH DESSERTS

The French culture is world-famous for its delicious desserts. A French wedding would feature tables piled high with these treats, to savor over cups of coffee while the music played.

Crème Brûlée

One of the most famous of French desserts is Crème Brûlée. The name is actually the French term for 'burnt cream'. In essence a custard is cooked, then cooled down. Sugar is sprinkled over the top of the custard, and a small torch is then used to caramelize it. The top of this delicacy should be crisp and warm, while the bottom is cool. It's the combination of the hot-cool and the textures of crunch-smooth that make this dish so interesting.

2 ½ cups heavy cream
4 large eggs
1/3 cup super fine sugar

Gently warm the cream and boil it for 30 seconds. Separate the yolks of the 4 eggs and whisk them into the cream. Simmer until the mixture thickens. Pour the custard into a shallow dish and refrigerate for 24 hours.

Before serving, sprinkle a layer of sugar over the top of the custard. Use a small blowtorch to quickly caramelize the sugar to a crunchy brown layer. You can also do this with a broiler set to high if you watch it carefully, and ensure the dish is oven safe.

Traditional Crème Brûlée is served plain, without any flavoring. However, it's become very popular to provide a variety of flavors – from vanilla to chocolate, Grand Marnier to Baileys, cinnamon to nutmeg to strawberry. You might consider putting out a selection of flavored Crème Brûlées, each labeled, and letting your guests choose their favorites!

Madelines

Madelines are famous French cookies. They are so famous there is even a young girl of the same name who is the heroine of several French children's books!

Madelines are very tasty and perfect with a cup of coffee or cocoa. 2 1/2 tsp ground ginger

2 tsp ground cinnamon
1 tsp ground nutmeg
3/4 tsp ground cardamom
3/4 tsp ground cloves
1/8 tsp salt
3 1/2 oz semisweet chocolate
3/4 cup unsalted butter
1/2 cup white sugar
1/4 cup brown sugar
5 large eggs; lightly beaten
1 1/2 cups all-purpose flour; sifted

In a small bowl, mix together the ginger, cinnamon, nutmeg, cardamom, cloves, and salt. In a small pot, melt the chocolate and butter together until smooth. In a large bowl, mix the chocolate and butter with brown and white sugar, then mix in the spices. Mix in the eggs, then mix in the flour.

Put the batter into traditional greased molds, and bake for 12 minutes at 350°F.

Croquembouche

The croquembouche is a pyramid of cream-filled pastries, reminiscent of that original pastry-pile which grew into the wedding cake. The cream-filled pastries are usually piled around a cone-shaped base and then 'glued' in place with a caramel syrup.

Cream Puff Dough:
1 cup water
½ cup unsalted butter 1 cup flour
1 tsp sugar
¼ tsp salt 4 eggs

Filling:
6 egg yolks
2 cups milk
½ cup sugar
¼ cup flour
⅛ tsp salt
1 tsp vanilla

Caramel Glue:
2 ½ cups sugar
¼ cup water

Mix together the water and butter, and bring to a boil in a saucepan. Add in the flour, sugar and salt. Lower heat to simmer and stir until the dough is a non-soggy lump. Let cool. Blend in eggs well. Put blend into a pastry bag and create puffs around ¾" across on parchment paper. Put on a cookie sheet and bake at 425° F for 25 minutes. Now cut a hole in the side of each and put back in the oven for a few minutes to dry out. Let cool

Now the filling. Blend together egg yolks, ½ cup milk, ¼ cup sugar, ¼ cup flour, and salt. Put remaining milk and sugar in a saucepan.

Bring to a simmer and add in the yolk blend. Keep stirring until thick, then cool. Stir in the vanilla after 5 minutes.

Finally, make the glue. Mix sugar and water in a saucepan and simmer. Stir until the color starts to turn brown. You're ready to begin assembly now.

Create a base for the pyramid, with either metal or foil cones. Fill each puff with the cream blend, using a pastry bag. Now start dipping each puff into the caramel mixture – enough to glue that particular puff into place. Make a ring around the base of the cone, and then start a second layer, and so on, putting the smaller puffs on the top. When done, sprinkle a glaze of any remaining caramel over the entire creation, to hold it into place.

French Apple Tart

The French are rightly famous for their fruit tarts, and this apple tart is sure to be a crowd pleaser.

Crust:
1 ¼ cup whole wheat flour
¼ tsp salt
5 Tbsp butter
5 Tbsp water

Apple Filling:
4 apples, sliced
2/3 cup cranberries

Topping:
4 Tbsp honey
3 Tbsp whole wheat flour
3 Tbsp butter
½ tsp cinnamon

Mix together flour and salt. Cut butter into small pieces and blend in thoroughly. Add in water, and mix well. Chill for an hour. Roll dough into 15" circle on wax paper. Blend apple slices and cranberries, and place in center of circle. Blend together honey, flour, butter and cinnamon, and sprinkle this topping over fruit mixture. Now bring dough up around edges of fruit, leaving an open hole in the middle. Bake on cookie sheet for 30 minutes at 450°F. Serve warm.

After The Reception

A French wedding reception could easily last into the next day, as celebrants continued to eat and drink. Eventually, though, the bride and groom would head to their new home together. This is where the 'chiverie' began. Chiverie were the pranks played on the bride and groom by their family and friends. These could include firing rifles in the old days, ringing bells, blowing horns, or banging pots and pans. The group would even sing ribald songs outside the couple's window.

The couple, showing how much they enjoy their family and friends, would then invite the group inside and they would all have more drinks and pastries.

As a modern chiverie, if the couple is traveling after the reception, many enjoy the tradition of tying cans to their car bumpers.

If the groom was a widower, some villages would make him pay a 'fine' for taking another wife. This was called 'la peloto', and would involve a party for all the unmarried men in the bride's village.

Living and Loving the French Way

It's easy to bring a touch of France to your own life – simply enjoy love, be romantic, and enjoy delicious foods and wines! For the French, these are the keys to happiness.

Food and Wine

The French know the contentment value of a delicious meal. It's easy to be satisfied with life when you have a belly full of delicious food, and a glass of fine wine in your hand. Neither needs to be very expensive either – most French people drink a "house wine" which comes from a local vineyard and is quite inexpensive.

Get to know the wineries of your home area, and talk to your local wine shop about great bargains. You can get some amazing wines for under ten dollars if you shop around.

Next, take some courses in cooking from your local community college, or get cookbooks from your local library and practice new dishes. Get fresh vegetables from your local farmers markets, and try a bread machine for fresh, homemade bread.

After an evening of great food and a good glass of wine, romance might come into your life quite naturally!

Music and Dining

The French are enthusiastic fans of getting out and being involved with people. Open-air seating is extremely popular, where you sit in the sun, sipping a glass of wine and watching the people walk by.

Nights out are popular as well, getting out to hear the local guitarists and musicians. The type of music doesn't matter – head out to a different tavern each week, and see what a wide range of talent is outside your doorstep. The fun is in experiencing the world of music, and seeing the range of people that are drawn to it.

Love and Romance

For the French, love and romance aren't restricted to first dates or heavy courtship periods. They are the way that life is lived. The French man would compliment the women around him whether they were 18 or 80, and make each one feel appreciated. The French woman would flirt with the grocery store clerk and the bank teller, enjoying the interaction with each. Their best glances would be saved for each other, to show each other that while they still enjoy the world at large, they have found their true match already.

The French do not equate money with love–expensive flowers are never a substitute for real affection and time spent on each other. While the French do enjoy flowers, they would be saved for special occasions, not for every day purchases, unless the family was so wealthy that it was an inconsequential expense. The French would rather grow flowers in their garden, to have them for free every day, and to be able to flirt in their presence.

Poetry is also free, and much loved by the French. A creative lover could write poetry specifically for a given situation or event, while more pragmatic individuals could simply select from a book of verses. Poems could be signed with flower drawings, providing a 'virtual bouquet'. Love notes are easy to slip to each other in a variety of ways.

You could serenade your love with the instrument of your choice, or gather a collection of your favorite songs and arrange them on a CD in the background. Being a French lover is not about being perfect–it is about being passionate and *caring* enough to try your best. It is the effort and the intention that are appreciated and respected.

French Hobbies

A hobby enjoyed by many French people is winemaking. It seems that every French person you meet is making some sort of wine, from grape wines to apple wine, dandelion wine, and even peach and plum wine.

There are many kits out there to help you get started. These kits include everything you need. If you're fortunate enough to have fruit trees in your back yard, or even berry bushes, you have the basic ingredients close at hand.

Dandelion Wine

One traditional, easy to make wine is Dandelion Wine. This would be made each spring when the dandelions were in bloom, and drunk either on the Winter solstice or the following May Day. Make some while you're engaged, and drink the fruits of your labor during your wedding reception!

4 quarts dandelion heads
2 gallons water
3 lemons
3 large oranges
2 lb white sugar
2 lb dark brown sugar
12 oz clover honey
2 lb golden raisins
1 package yeast
1 piece bread, toasted

Pick the dandelions at mid-day when the blooms are wide open. Completely remove the stalks and leaves, but it is fine to leave on the little green under-petals. Put the flowers into a ceramic bowl. Boil the water, and pour it into the bowl over the flowers. Cover tightly with plastic wrap.

Let the mixture sit for two days, being sure to remove the plastic and stir it twice each day. Put the mix into a pot and boil again. Peel the oranges and lemons and then break the peels up into large pieces. Into the pot, add the sugar, honey, lemon peels and orange peels. Boil for an hour. Return to a ceramic pot and add in the juice & pulp of lemons and oranges. Let stand until cool. Spread the yeast onto the toast, and then place the piece of toast on the top of the liquid, floating. Cover the container, and let it stand for three days.

Strain the mixture and put the liquid into a fermentation vessel – glass is preferred. Add in raisins and top with an airlock – something that lets extra air out, but doesn't let air in easily. Leave the blend to ferment until any bubbling stops. Then rack out the sediment and bottle the wine. Dandelion wine is drinkable after six months, but tastes best after a year of aging.

French Baby Names

Whether it's a new boy or girl coming into your life, a pet, or even a new boat, here are some French names to consider!

Aimee: loved
Alberta: noble
Alexandre: defender
Arielle: strength of God
August: noble
Aurore: dawn
Beau: handsome
Bernadette: brave
Brigette: strong
Bruce: woods
Carol: joyful song
Claire: clear
Darci: fortress
Darlene: little darling
Evette: young archer
Fleur: flower
Fontaine: fountain
Forrest: forest
Gabrielle: devoted to God
Gervaise: honorable
Isabelle: consecrated to God
Juliet: youthful
Kurt: courteous
Lyle: island
Nadia: hopeful
Olivier: the olive tree
Sherry: beloved
Virginie: pure

French Movies

France, with its romance, grand history, and gorgeous costumes throughout the ages, makes a perfect location to shoot movies. Tales can be told about the courtly excesses, about the chaos of the revolution, and about the romance and music of modern days. Rent a French movie, slice some cheese, grab a bottle of Champagne, and be swept away!

Un Air de Famille
Winner of numerous awards, this drama is an extremely insightful look into family members and how they interact with each other.

Amélie
Amélie is the title character who enjoys fixing the lives of others. She tempts her father, who really wants to travel, by sending his garden gnome on various adventures. She eventually has her own romance to tend to. There are gorgeous scenes of Montmartre.

An American in Paris
Gene Kelly is an American soldier who, after WWII, decides to stay in Paris and become an artist. He must decide between loving a rich American woman and a younger French woman who is already engaged to another. There is lots of singing and dancing, including the famous song "I Got Rhythm."

An American Werewolf in Paris
This is the sequel to An American Werewolf in London. The movie is full of violence and special effects, and gives you glimpses of the Paris landscapes.

Antoine and Colette
Antoine is an 18 year old who is infatuated with Colette. He attempts to woo her despite her continual rebuffs.

Auntie Danielle

Auntie Danielle moves in with her nephew and his wife, who hope that their children will benefit from spending time with the older generation. However, Auntie's demands and harsh attitude bring great trouble to the family.

Babette's Feast
This is a gorgeous tale of two sisters who pass by romance for a life serving God, and the cook who creates a scrumptious feast for them after winning the lottery.

The Baker's Wife
A couple settle into a quiet town and take over the local bakery. The wife runs off with her lover, and the desolate husband can't find the will to bake bread any more. The village bands together to get their bread back and bring the wife back to her husband.

Belle de jour
A bored housewife from Paris discovers a brothel nearby, and starts going there during the day when her husband is away. The movie is very seductive without any explicit sex scenes.

Breathless
This tale of young love involves the Parisian boy stealing a car and killing a police officer. They then roam the streets of Paris planning an escape to Italy.

The Bride Wore Black
Jeanne Moreau is the title character in this story of revenge. She is married to the man she loves, but as they leave the church, he is shot and killed. Jeanne then dedicates her life to tracking down and killing all involved in the murder of her husband.

Brotherhood of the Wolf
Set in the 18th century, a scientist and American Indian pursue a gigantic wolf that is terrorizing France.

La Buche
A Christmas holiday story, two parents bring their three grown daughters home for the holidays. The family ends up revealing a

lot of information to each other that had been hidden for years.

Camille Claudel
Camille Claudel was a famous sculptor in France in the late 1800's. The movie shows her digging her own clay, and crafting beautiful sculptures. The movie portrays her love affair with the artist Rodin, and her descent into madness.

Children of Paradise
Set in Paris in the 1800's, the story traces a theater company where many are in love with the actress. The plot boasts quite a combination of characters.

Chocolate
Chocolate is a scrumptious tale of love set in France in the late 1950's. Juliette Binoche plays a single mother who comes to a quiet village with her daughter to open a chocolate shop. Unfortunately it's a time of fasting, which pits the young woman against the local church. The town doesn't approve of her single lifestyle. Judi Dench shines as the mother, and Johnny Depp plays the gypsy lover.

The Closet
A man working at a condom manufacturer discovers that he's about to be let go. He decides that if he's a homosexual his boss won't be able to fire him, so he sets up elaborate ruses to convince his co-workers that he prefers men.

The Count of Monte Cristo
Written by Alexander Dumas (of The Three Musketeers fame), a man named Dantes is wrongfully imprisoned for 13 years. When he is freed, he weaves a web of revenge against those who placed him there. The 2001 version was filmed in Malta and Ireland.

Diary of a Chambermaid
A Paris girl comes to work in the French countryside for a family, and is upset when the girl of the household is murdered. She delves into the situation, trying to figure out what happened.

The Eighth Day
A strong friendship builds up between two very special men. One of

the men has Down's syndrome, and the actor who plays him –
Pascal Duquenne – does actually have Down's syndrome.

East West
After World War II, a family moves from France to Russia to get a
new start on life. They realize quickly that the grass isn't always
greener on the other side.

Entres Nous
Two women decide to leave their husbands, and are drawn to each
other. The story tells how the two marriages dissolve, and how the
friendship between the women deepens.

Forget Paris
Forget Paris is an interesting modern tale in which Billy Crystal
and Deborah Winger meet while Billy Crystal is trying to bury his
father with his D-day platoon. The two fall in love and marry. Much
of the movie is told at a dinner party, as all of the friends
remember bits and pieces of the courtship and marriage.

The Four Musketeers (Oliver Reed)
This sequel to the Three Musketeers reunites the main characters in
yet another set of complications with M'Lady DeWinter, Cardinal
Richelieu, and the Duke of Buckingham.

The 400 Blows
The first movie directed by Francois Truffaut. This is a tale of young
Antoine who is neglected at home, and turns to a life of crime.

French Kiss
Meg Ryan's boyfriend leaves her for a French beauty, and Meg wants
him back. Afraid of flying, she turns to Kevin Kline for help on her
mission. Lots of French scenery and charm help shore up an
unevenly plotted movie.

The French Lieutenant's Woman
Meryl Streep and Jeremy Irons star in this fascinating tale of a
woman who is incorrectly labeled as a fallen woman, and a man
who deliberately falls to be with her. At the same time, the story tells

of the actress playing the woman, who is married, having an affair with the actor playing the man.

The Grand Illusion
In World War I, three French officers try to escape from a German prison. The German upper class soldier feels a kinship with the noble Frenchman even though they are on different sides of a political conflict.

Hate
This rough story is an urban tale of racism and class struggle. It is set in Paris and follows three friends as they try to survive in a rough world.

Henry V
While the movie begins in England, the vast majority of this Shakespeare classic takes place on the battlefields of France. The Olivier version is more of a period piece, while the Brannagh version gets you down into the mud and pain of the tortured tale. The St. Crispan's Day speech in both is a treat!

The Hunchback of Notre Dame (1939)
This movie is heralded by many as the best version of the classic Victor Hugo story. Charles Laughton plays the Hunchback as a gruesome character that all revile. He falls for the beautiful

Esmerelda, played by Maureen O'Hara. It is a must-see, especially for those who have only seen the cartoon version.

The Hunchback of Notre Dame (Disney)
Disney's cartoon version of the tale changes the characters, storyline and especially the ending so it's more kid-friendly. Quasimodo, the happy, singing hunchback, falls for the gypsy Esmerelda. She loves one of the king's guards. The evil Frollo, a monk, loves Esmerelda and decides to kill her rather than see her with another. This is an interesting tale, but not true to the real story.

Interview with a Vampire
Tom Cruise and Brad Pitt star in this tale of despair and vampires. Part of the story is based in gothic France.

Irma Vep
In a tale about filmmaking that was inspired after a film festival, the lead character goes through various troubles trying to get a film through its life cycle.

Jean de Florette
Based on the famous French novel, this movie tells of two farmers in the 1920's who are engaged in a rivalry. One is a simple farmer, the other a greedy one. The sequel to this was Manon of the Spring.

Jules and Jim
The film most associated with director François Truffaut, the story tells of a beautiful young woman during WWI in Paris, and her best friend, Jules. She also has a great friendship with Jim, a writer, and although she marries Jules, she still involves Jim in her life, and the love triangle wreaks havoc.

The Gleaners and I
This plot is a comparison of the huge amount of excess food and material that many in our world create, and how this excess is "gleaned" by others as their sole method of living.

La Cage Aux Folles
This classic was the basis for "The Birdcage" starring Robin Williams. The movie tells of a gay couple who must masquerade as a man and wife when their son brings home a straight-laced fiancée.

Ladyhawke
Matthew Broderick, Michelle Pfeiffer, and Rutger Hauer star in this medieval tale of magic. Michelle and Rutger are lovers who have been doomed never to be together—each day Michelle is turned into a hawk, and each night Rutger is turned into a wolf. The three team up to break the spell and bring contentment to the pair.

The Last Metro
Nominated for best foreign language Oscar in 1980, this story is based during WWII and tells of the Theater Montmarte. The Jewish owner hides in the basement while the theater struggles to stay alive.

A great romance.

The Last Tango in Paris
Marlon Brando stars in a film which was properly called shocking at
its release in 1973. The character's wife has just committed suicide
and he retreats into a very sexual but emotionally distant
relationship with a young Parisian woman.

Madame Bovary
Based on the famous novel, the wife of Dr. Bovary finds no
happiness in her family or belongings, and tries to bring excitement to
her life through lovers. She finds that they do not intrigue her either,
not realizing that her own outlook on life is the real problem.

Le Magnifique
Francois is a novelist who suddenly becomes embroiled in a real
life spy adventure. A great comedy based on the spy genre, and the
predecessor for Austin Powers.

Man in the Iron Mask
Based on the story by Alexandre Dumas, this tale tells of King

Louis XIV, who locks his twin brother in prison with an iron mask so
that his rule can never be overthrown. John Malkovich is the elderly
Athos who gathers his musketeer friends together to free the jailed
prince.

Manon of the Spring
Sequel of Jean de Florette, this story tells of the daughter of the
doomed farmer from the first movie, and her revenge on the greedy
farmer who caused his downfall.

Marius and Jeannette
Jeannette is a single mom trying desperately to keep her family
afloat. She meets Marius, and slowly their friendship grows into
something stronger.

Le Million
This fantastic comedy is a classic. It tells of a poor, starving artist
who wins a lottery, but somehow loses track of the ticket.

Les Miserables
A classic by Victor Hugo that has been filmed several times. A prisoner, Jean Valjean, is locked up for almost 20 years for stealing bread. He is finally released and tries to forge a new life, but a former prison guard makes it difficult. Avoid the Liam Neeson version which turns the story into a teen romance.

Moulin Rougue
A love story with an unusual combination of eras. Nicole Kidman stars as the woman desired by two men, she must choose between her pocketbook and her heart. Lots of song and dance.

My Father's Glory
Based on the life story of French poet Marcel Pagnol, this movie traces his early years. Gorgeous footage of the Provençal landscape. Note that there was a sequel, My Mother's Castle.

My Life to Live
A Paris salesgirl leaves her husband and longs to be an actress, but winds up as a prostitute. Done documentary style in twelve parts.

The Phantom of the Opera
This classic has been a movie, a television miniseries, and a musical. The tale tells of a man who lives in Paris' sewers because he is disfigured and shunned by society. He loves a beautiful opera singer, who falls in love with both him and another man. The television miniseries is well acclaimed.

The Return of Martin Guerre
This romance is based in medieval France, during the Hundred Years' War. Martin Guerre is a soldier who returns to his wife and village after a long absence. He is much changed, so much so that the village feels he is an imposter. The wife, however, is extremely pleased with this kinder, gentler version of her husband and wishes to keep him.

The Son of Gascogne
This 1995 movie is in French with English subtitles, and tells of a

teenage boy who is suddenly very popular because various movie stars and famous people think he's the son of 'Gascogne'. His mother refuses to tell him if this is true, and he enjoys the attention.

The Scarlet Pimpernel
There have been many, many versions of this story filmed. Each covers the basic storyline. The time is the French Revolution, and a foppish English lord has gathered together a band of friends to help save the French nobility from the guillotine. His French-born wife knows nothing of this, and is bribed by the French government to track down and reveal the identity of the Scarlet Pimpernel.

Shoot the Piano Player
Charlie is a piano player in a low-rate bar in Paris, hiding from his past as a great concert pianist. His brother is hiding from a few criminals. A fun film noir to watch with a friend.

Small Change
Children in a French village go through their normal trials and tribulations in a movie which many herald as a completely true vision of what childhood is about.

The Soft Skin
This Hitchcockian tale by director François Truffaut follows a married publisher who has an affair with a flight attendant he sees during his frequent trips. The relationships unravel when he is discovered.

Stolen Kisses
Sequel to The 400 Blows, this story continues with Antoine and his new object of desire, Christine. Full of romantic comedy and sweetness.

The Story of Adele H
The daughter of Victor Hugo, Adele Hugo became obsessed with a French soldier and tried to force him to love her. She failed, but the tale of her obsession becomes an interesting character change to watch.

Summer

A young woman from Paris is abandoned for the summer and tries to find ways to occupy her time, with little success. Finally, at the point of giving up, she stumbles into romance.

The Three Muskeeteers (Oliver Reed)
I could never tire of watching this movie. Oliver Reed, Michael York and Richard Chamberlain star as members of the Musketeers who must protect the Queen's honor from the plots of the Cardinal. Lots of great sword-fighting, and of course the delightful Raquel Welch.

The Three Musketeers (Disney)
Starring Keifer Sutherland and Charlie Sheen, this watered-down version has the Queen suddenly completely faithful and in love with her husband, and D'Artagnan's loves a single maiden. A lot of the intrigue is therefore missing and it's a simple rescue-the-girl mission with some truly great lines.

Les Triplettes de Bellevelle
Winner of many awards, this 2003 animated film has great characters and even better music.

Ma Vie en Rose
Ludovic is a young boy who is convinced he wants to be a girl instead, to wear pretty clothes and dress up. His schoolmates and even the adults around him react with anger and disgust.

The Widow of Saint-Pierre
A man on a remote French island is sentenced to death by guillotine, but unfortunately the island doesn't have one. While the many years pass in which the guillotine is ordered, the jailer's wife and then the jailer as well both work on helping the prisoner become a better person.

A Woman is a Woman
A striptease artist wants to have a child, but her boyfriend refuses. She turns to his best friend and trouble ensues.

The Woman Next Door
Gerard Depardieu stars in this tale of romance blossoming anew.
Two former lovers meet up by accident and although both have ended
up marrying a suitable partner, it is plain that the current pairings
do not match the intensity of what they had before.

Visiting France

France presents such a wide range of landscapes and things to do that there's sure to be something for everyone! From the gorgeous beaches of the Mediterranean to the delicious wines of Champagne, Bordeaux and Burgundy, from hot air ballooning to leisurely canal rides, from the museums of Paris to the fishing and golfing, France is sure to please.

One of the keys to enjoying France is not to rush. France is about relaxing, taking your time. It's about sipping a glass of wine at an open air café, watching the people that stroll by on the cobblestone street. It's about lounging on a beach at the French Riviera, watching the clouds float by as a yacht sails along the ocean. It's about drifting down the canal in a house-barge, talking with the farmer and buying fresh cheese from him before moving along to the next lock.

Relax, and enjoy the sights and sounds of France!

Champagne and Reims

Reims is the central city in the region of Champagne – the one place in the world where true sparkling Champagne comes from. There is the gorgeous Cathedral of Notre-Dame to visit and hundreds of Champagne wineries to explore.

The Notre-Dame Cathedral, also called Cathedral of Our Lady, was begun in 1211. This cathedral saw the coronation of many French kings, and is one of the finest gothic cathedrals to be found in Europe. The church's involvement in coronations was begun by Archbishop St Remi (440-553), and his remains are in the church. The church was built on the location that French kings were traditionally crowned. The Cathedral was severely damaged during both WWI and WWII, but has been repaired each time. Note that this is a different cathedral from the Notre Dame Cathedral in Paris, which the famous story is written about.

I love Reims and definitely recommend at least a few days in this area to soak it all in.

Many of the Champagne wineries do not allow visitors, as they are small, working farms without enough staff to handle questions and tastings. Still, the larger wineries do offer tours and tastings. While it might be fun to visit during the harvest season in September and October, remember that some wineries shut down all tourist activities during those busy times. Be sure to check with your favorite wineries to see if you can learn more about how they create the Drink of Celebrations!

Champagne Charles Heidsieck 4, boulevard Henry Vasnier Tel : 33/03 26 84 43 50

Champagne Krug 5, rue Coquebert

Tel. 33/3 26 84 44 20

Champagne Lanson 66, rue de Courlancy Tel. 33/3 26 78 50 50

Champagne Maxim's 17, rue des Créneaux Tel. 33/3 26 82 70 67

Champagne Mercier 20 Avenue Champagne

Champagne G.H. Mumm & Cie 34, rue du Champ de Mars
Tel. 33/3 26 49 59 70

Champagne Laurent Perrier 51150 Tours-sur-Marne

Tel. 33/3 26 58 91 22

Champagne Perrier-Jouet Tel. 33/3 26 53 38 10

Champagne Piper-Heidsieck 51, bd Henry Vasnier

Tel. 33/3 26 84 43 44

Champagne Pommery

5 place du Général Gouraud Tel. 33/3 26 61 62 56

Champagne Ruinart 4, rue des Crayères Tel. 33/3 26 77 51 51

Champagne Louis Roederer 21, bd Lundy

Tel. 33/3 26 40 42 11

Champagne Taittinger 9 place Saint-Nicaise

Tel. 33/3 26 85 84 33

Champagne Veuve Clicquot Ponsardin 1, place des Droits de
l'Homme

Tel. 33/3 26 89 53 90

Paris - City of Love

If you ask a person what city most embodies love and romance, it's likely that many times the answer will be "Paris." Paris is the capital city of France, known for its beautiful riverbanks, its friendly cafes, its museums full of famous artwork and its bars full of music.

Most cities only have one river, but Paris has three – the Seine, the Marne, and the Oise. Around these rivers rise several hills, each forming an area with a distinct personality. Montmartre is known for its music.

The Cathedral at Notre-Dame was the famous location for the "Hunchback of Notre Dame" story, and boasts magnificent architecture. It is located on the Ile de la Cité, a small island formed by the converging rivers. It was begun in 1163 and became the model on which other cathedrals were based. It was heavily damaged during the French Revolution and some parts of it were only restored as recently as 2001.

The Louvre Museum contains many of the world's greatest paintings and sculptures. Begun as a fortress in 1190, the Louvre now contains the Mona Lisa by Leonardo da Vinci, the Venus de Milo sculpture, Winged Victory, and many other famous works.

The Opéra de Paris Garnier was built in the late 1800s, and is the location of the famous play *Phantom of the Opera*. It is the largest theater in the world based on square footage, and is known both for the ballets it produces as well as its magnificent architecture.

One of the most famous structures in Paris is the Eiffel Tower. Built in 1889 for the International Exposition of Paris, the tower celebrated 100 years of democracy in France. The architect was Gustave Eiffel, and at the time it was the tallest building in the world. It was intended to be taken down in 1909, but by then it was being used as a large antenna. Since then, it has become the most well-known monument in Europe.

Another stop near Paris is the Palace of Versailles. This was the home of the French royalty from the late 1600's to late 1700's. It is famous for its hall of mirrors and extensive gardens. Much of it was looted during the French Revolution, and it is now a historic site.

There are thousands of other places to visit in the Paris region. If you head out to this area of France, be sure to grab a guide book and learn more!

Bordeaux Wine Region

The Bordeaux wines are considered by many to be some of the finest wines in the world, and a bottle of Bordeaux can easily go for a hundred dollars or more. In comparison, tasting the wines at the winery is extremely inexpensive and fun! A trip to the beautiful landscapes and vineyards of the Bordeaux region could prove to be an enjoyable and relaxing way to visit the French countryside.

The best wines in this region are known as "First Growths", and typically command the most money per bottle. If you are able to get to one of these wineries, it's well worth the visit! There are also hundreds of other wineries which can be quite interesting to tour and taste at.

First Growths (Premiers Crus) of Medoc (red) Bordeaux (1855):

Château Lafite-Rothschild (Pauillac)

Château Margaux (Margaux)

Château Latour (Pauillac)

Château   Haut-BrionPessac   (Graves)

(included because of its greatness)

Château Mouton-Rothschild (Pauillac)

First Growths (Premiers Crus) Classés of St-Émilion (1985):

Château Ausone

Château Cheval Blanc

If you can't get out to the Bordeaux region, try these classic drink recipes involving the Bordeaux wines, and take a virtual trip!

Claret Cup

This classic recipe was enjoyed long before 1877, and was popular at dinner parties. Claret is the British term for Bordeaux.

Mix one quart of claret, one bottle of soda water, one lemon cut very thin, four tablespoons of powdered sugar, one quarter of a teaspoon of grated nutmeg, one liqueur glass of brandy, one wine glass of sherry wine. Half an hour before it is used, put in a large piece of ice, so that it may get perfectly cold.

From *The Home Cook Book*, 1877

Mint Julep

From the Fannie Farmer cookbook of 1918. Popular in the southern US.

1 quart water

1 cup orange juice

2 cups sugar

Juice of 8 lemons

1 pint claret wine (Bordeaux)

1 1/2 cups boiling water

1 cup strawberry juice

12 sprigs fresh mint

Make syrup by boiling quart of water and sugar twenty minutes. Separate mint in pieces, add to the boiling water, cover, and let stand in warm place five minutes, strain, and add to syrup; add fruit juices, and cool. Pour into punch-bowl, add claret, and chill with a large piece of ice; dilute with water. Garnish with fresh mint leaves and whole strawberries.

Cannes / Beaches of Southern France

The French Riviera may seem like a spot for the trendy rich and famous, but it's been sought after by travelers since the days of the ancient Greeks. This region of France has not only gorgeous beaches, but also museums, ruins, and beautiful landscapes. Its beauty inspired the painters Van Gogh and Cezanne, and is equally lush today.

The beaches of the French Riviera receive 10 million visitors a year, making them one of the 5 most popular places to visit in the world. Saint Tropez is a resort town known for its blue waters and people-watching.

One of the most famous events in southern France is the Festival de Cannes, or the Cannes Film Festival. Begun in 1946, this month-long tribute to world filmmaking takes place each May. It's difficult to get in to the actual events, but it can be great fun to be in the area and see the stars and celebrities wander around town.

The town of Nice is a quiet place with cobblestone stairs and Roman ruins. Rent a bed and breakfast and enjoy a glass of wine in a flower-filled garden, while the world strolls by.

Châteauneuf-du-Pape, a red wine whose heritage traces to the 14th century Papal Chateau, is grown in this region. It is thought by some to be the finest red wine in the world. There's also the Palais des Papes, or Palace of the Popes, a fortress tracing to the 14th century as well.

Monte Carlo and Monaco

Monaco is less than two miles wide and covers a square mile in land. With only 30,000 residents, it is one of the smallest countries around. In fact, about a quarter of its current land mass was reclaimed from the sea in the past 20 years. It is so crowded that in order to build a new building, an old one would first have to be torn down. It is completely surrounded by France and is extremely closely tied to the French culture.

Monte Carlo is one of Monaco's few towns, and its most famous one. The Grimaldi family took control of this small area in 1295, and the country has struggled ever since to maintain its independence from its neighbors. Prince Ranier is currently the ruler of Monaco. The country draws most of its laws from France – Prince Ranier receives signed legislation from the President of France, to then approve or disapprove of for his own small country. France is in fact responsible for defending the area.

Monaco has become a haven for the wealthy, as there is no income tax and very low business tax. Its world-famous casinos, restaurants and shops attract well-to-do visitors from around the globe.

Most visitors stop in Monte Carlo as part of a cruise along the Mediterranean, or as a side trip from another location in France. While it is extremely expensive to stay and eat in this small nation, it is a gorgeous place to visit, and offers sights not seen anywhere else in the world. I love the Japanese garden. The zoo is also fun to pop in and visit.

Splurge in Monaco for a day, and go see how the wealthy live!

The Canals of France

France is a country of rivers and canals, many of the canals dating from the 17th century. Created initially to help barge traffic move goods around the country, they now provide a peaceful way for tourists to experience the real world of French life. If you're planning a trip to France, a wonderful way to see the countryside is to rent a barge and move at your own pace down the canals.

One main canal system traces from Bordeaux down to the Mediterranean, passing near Toulouse. Another system heads north from the coast through Lyon and into Paris and other northeastern areas. All canals were set up deliberately to allow easy passage from one to the other, so with very little trouble you can wend your way through much of the French countryside, relaxing and enjoying life.

You can choose to go on a barge with a chef, and be pampered, savoring a new meal each day. If you'd like to be on your own, you can rent your own barge and enjoy the freedom of travel. There are plenty of pastry shops, coffee houses and restaurants along the canals, so stopping for wine and cheese is never a problem.

The residents along the canals are very friendly and love to chat with the boaters. Boaters talk with each other as well, sharing stories and memories. You can only go 3 mph in the canal system, so there is not much danger of getting lost or damaged. You simply drift along, adjusting to the French speed of life.

Depending on what else you want to see in France, you can use the canals as a way of getting from place to place, or as the focus as the trip – to see what France is really like.

Glossary of French Terms

Affaire du Coeur: An affair of the heart Alliance: wedding ring

Amant: lover

Au Revoir: until I see you again A votre sante: to your health!

Boutonniere: A flower worn by the groom, to show his tie to the bride

Carre: silk canopy which a bride and groom stand beneath in the church while the priest marries them.

C'est la vie: such is life

Chiverie: wedding night pranks played on the new bride and groom.

Copain: boyfriend Copine: girlfriend

Coupe de Marriage: a two-handled cup from which the bride and groom drink together.

Crème Brûlée: literally 'burnt cream', this famous French dessert combines counterbalanced textures and flavors.

Croquembouche: a pyramid of cream-filled pastries

Dragées: almonds coated in chocolate, a traditional treat at weddings. They symbolize that marriage has both sweet and bitter parts to it.

Embrassez-moi: kiss me En Rapport: in agreement

Entre Nous: between ourselves Famille: family

Femme: wife Finacailles: engagement

Jarretière: the bride's garter, thrown to the crowd during the reception.

Je t'aime: I love you

Joie de vivre: thrill of being alive Mari: husband

Mariage: marriage Marie: married Noces: wedding

Rendez-vous: Meeting arrangement

Trousseau: the hope chest and other items a bride would bring with her to the marriage

Veux-tu m'epouser?: Will you marry me?

Web Resources

General French Information

http://www.discoverfrance.net
A collection of pages on French wine, skiing, travel, history and much more.

http://frenchculture.bellaonline.com/
The French Culture site offers reviews of things to see and do in France.

http://www.romanceclass.com
A romantic site that covers the customs of many countries, including France.

French Merchants

http://www.munnwerks.com/frenchpottery
French pottery from all regions of the country, focusing on Alsace.

http://www.levillage.com
Traditional French cheese, chocolates, meats, and much more.

http://www.craftsfrance.com
This website has a collection of French artists, with wares from pottery to paintings to much more.

http://www.thefrenchhouse.net
Everything you need to decorate your home in a French style, from glassware for the kitchen to decorations for your bath.

French Travel

http://www.francetourism.com
The homepage for French Tourism, this website has a great deal of information about the French culture.

http://us.franceguide.com
Guide to travel in france by type of activity and area of visitation.

http://www.alltravelfrance.com
A one stop travel center with information on hotels, car rentals, train, bus and other systems a visitor needs to understand.

Champagne Websites

http://www.wineintro.com
Information on how to open Champagne, including how to pour, serve, and tasting notes.

http://www.champagne-boizel.fr
Boizel Champagnes
The Boizel House purchases grapes from some 70 different crus. This diversity enables blending from a very wide selection and provides the complexity which confers the character on Boizel wines which is so sought after by champagne lovers.

http://www.champagne-boulard.fr
Raymond Boulard
The Boulard family has been tending their vines for five generations, since 1792. Today, they farm land in seven villages, including top ranking Grand Cru on the hillside of the Marne Valley and Montagne de Reims.

http://www.vinternet.net/LeclercBriant
Champagne Leclerc Briant
The village of Cumières enjoys a micro climate which favours the early ripening of the grapes. As a matter of fact, the grape picking in Champagne starts every year in Cumières for the black skinned grapes of Pinot Noir and Pinot Meunier.

http://www.castellane.com
Champagne de Castellane
De Castellane chooses grapes which come from the best vineyards of the Montagne de Reims, the Marne Valley, Côte des Blancs and the Aube district.

http://www.epicuria.fr/jm-rigot/index.htm
J.M. Rigot Champagne
Site in French only, J.M. Rigot has been around for five centuries.

http://www.jacquart-champagne.fr
Jacquart
Jacquart has 1,000 hectares of vineyards lain in the most prestigious soils of the Champagne District: Grande montagne de Reims, Vallée de la Marne, and Côte des Blancs.

http://www.lanson.tm.fr/english/lanson.htm
Lanson
Founded in 1760, Lanson is one of the oldest Champagne Houses. At this period in time, the Maltese cross became the emblem of the House in homage to its founder, also a knight in that order.

http://www.champagnemercier.com/
Champagne Mercier
The best selling Champange within France, and the most popular tour in Reims.

http://www.moet.com
Moet & Chandon
The wine merchant Claude Moët founded the House of Moët in Épernay in 1743. Today, 1 in every 4 bottles exported from the Champagne region comes from Moët & Chandon, which is the leading brand in most world markets.

http://www.perrier-jouet.com/
Perrier-Jouet
Famous for their flower bottle label, Perrier Jouet makes some of the finest Champagnes available.

http://www.piper.heidsieck.com
Piper-Heidsieck Champagne
Site is in French only. Piper-Heidsieck was founded in 1785 and is well known for its Bruts.

http://www.taittinger.com
Taittinger
In 1734, Jacques Fourneaux founded the company that was to become Taittinger. Taittinger is one of the last of the great concerns to bear the name of the family that in fact manages it.

Dedication

This book is dedicated to my darling, wonderful partner, Bob See. Bob and I have been together for twenty years. Bob's heritage is French – the See name originally traces to Huguenots who fled France in the seventeenth century to settle in the Hudson Valley region of New York.

I wish to thank these individuals who made Weddings and Courtships: France possible:

Jody Zolli, Jenn Mottram, Maureen O'Brien, Shirley Starke, Bob See, and Debi Gardiner.

About the Author

Lisa Shea is very fond of the beauty and grace of France. From the Mediterranean coastlines to the historic chateaus, there is something in every corner of France to delight and please. For wine lovers, there are Champagnes, Bordeauxs and Burgundies. For those who love history, there are paintings and architecture. For those who simply want to relax, France offers a quiet, peaceful way of life.

Lisa has been to France many times, to soak in the culture, visit the wineries, enjoy the museums, and simply enjoy life.

One of Lisa's favorite memories of France involves spending several hours over a long, leisurely lunch in Paris, sipping wine and enjoying the conversation.

Lisa has been writing about romance since her school days, and it was inevitable that one of her first books on romantic traditions focuses on the multifaceted wonders of France.

The Wedding & Courtships series:

Weddings & Courtships: Ireland

http://www.weddingsandcourtships.com/ireland/

Weddings & Courtships: France

http://www.weddingsandcourtships.com/france/

Weddings & Courtships: Italy

http://www.weddingsandcourtships.com/italy/

Medieval romance novels:
Knowing Yourself
Seeking the Truth
Finding Peace
A Sense of Duty
Creating Memories
Looking Back
Badge of Honor
Lady in Red
Believing your Eyes
Trusting in Faith
Sworn Loyalty
In A Glance

Cozy romance murder mystery series:
Aspen Allegations | Birch Blackguards | Cedar Conundrums

Blackstone Valley mystery novelette series:
Rumble Strip

Sci-fi adventure romance series:
Aquarian Awakenings | Betelgeuse Beguiling | Centauri Chaos |
Draconis Discord

Dystopian journey series:
Into the Wasteland | He Who Was Living | Broken Images

Scottish regency time-travel series:
One Scottish Lass | A Time Apart | A Circle in Time

1800s Tennessee black / Native American series:
Across the River | In the Pines

Sci-fi and Massachusetts short stories:
Chartreuse | The Angst of Change | BAAC | Melting | Armsby

Black Cat short stories:
The Lucky Cat – Black Cat Vol. 1

Here are a few of Lisa's self-help books:

Yoga for Stress Relief and Forgiveness
Step by step guidance to improving your health and serenity

Journaling Basics – Journal Writing for Beginners
Everything you need to know to get started with journaling

Quick No-Cook Low Carb Recipes
Heathy, easy recipes with low sugar

Secrets to Falling Asleep
Get better sleep to improve health and reduce stress

Dream Symbol Encyclopedia
Interpretation and meaning of dream symbols

Lucid Dreaming Guide
Foster creativity in a lucid dream state

Learning to say NO – and YES! To your Dream
Protect your goals while gently helping others succeed

Reduce Stress Instantly
Practical relaxation tips you can use right now for instant stress relief

Time Management Course
Learn to end procrastination, increase productivity, and reduce stress

Simple Ways to Make the World Better for Everyone
Every day we wake up is a day to take a fresh path, to help a friend, and to improve our lives.

"Be the change you wish to see in the world."

www.ingramcontent.com/pod-product-compliance
Lightning Source LLC
Chambersburg PA
CBHW070655290526
45790CB00001B/329